PENGUIN BOOKS

FITS AND STARTS

Andrew Ward was born in Chicago in 1946. A former
contributing editor of the *Atlantic Monthly*, Mr. Ward
received the Fund for Animals' 1989 Genesis Award for
his commentaries on National Public Radio's *All Things
Considered*, many of which are included in his book *Out
Here: A Newcomer's Notes from the Great Northwest*.
His previous books include *The Blood Seed*, a novel, and
A Cry of Absence. Andrew Ward now lives with his
family on Bainbridge Island, near Seattle, Washington.

Fits and Starts

The Premature Memoirs of

Andrew Ward

PENGUIN BOOKS

PENGUIN BOOKS
Published by the Penguin Group
Viking Penguin, a division of Penguin Books USA Inc.,
375 Hudson Street, New York, New York 10014, U.S.A.
Penguin Books Ltd, 27 Wrights Lane,
London W8 5TZ, England
Penguin Books Australia Ltd, Ringwood,
Victoria, Australia
Penguin Books Canada Ltd, 10 Alcorn Avenue, Suite 300,
Toronto, Ontario, Canada M4V 3B2
Penguin Books (N.Z.) Ltd, 182–190 Wairau Road,
Auckland 10, New Zealand

Penguin Books Ltd, Registered Offices:
Harmondsworth, Middlesex, England

First published in the United States of America by
Little, Brown and Company in association with
The Atlantic Monthly Press 1978
This edition with a new preface published in Penguin Books 1991

1 3 5 7 9 10 8 6 4 2

Copyright © Andrew Ward, 1976, 1977, 1978, 1991
All rights reserved

"U-Turn," originally published under the title "The Sunday Drive: Dad Against
Fate," © 1976 by The New York Times Company, and "The Jerk," originally published under the title "A Soda Jerk's True Confessions," © 1977 by The New York
Times Company, are reprinted by permission of *The New York Times*. "Rub-Out,"
© 1976 by the Massachusetts Horticultural Society, appeared in *Horticulture*. "Lift
Your Feet," "Offsides," "The Last Mambo," "Pencils Down," and "With My Grandparents at an Inn: August 1970" appeared in *The Atlantic Monthly*.

The lyrics from "Try to Remember" from "The Fantasticks" are used by permission.
Copyright © 1960 by Tom Jones and Harvey Schmidt. Chappell & Co., Inc., admin-
istrator, of publication and allied rights throughout the world. International Copyright Secured. ALL RIGHTS RESERVED.

The Library of Congress has catalogued the hardcover as follows:
Ward, Andrew, 1946–
Fits and starts: the premature memoirs of.
"An Atlantic Monthly Press book."
1. Ward, Andrew, 1946– 2. United States—
Biography. I. Title.
CT275.W27446A33 973.92'092'4 [B] 77–18850
ISBN 0-316-92199-8 (hc.)
ISBN 0 14 01.3055 1 (pbk.)

Printed in the United States of America
Set in Caslon
Designed by Chris Benders

Contents

Author's Note

My complexion began to clear up this year, and I bought myself a sweater vest, so it seemed a good time to write my memoirs. It's a lucky thing I got them out of the way before anyone told me that one of the requirements of a good memoirist is a good memory. As it is, I have managed to get around my inability to remember names, dates, places, and where I last saw my car keys only by playing fast and loose with the facts.

I have a lot of people I want to thank, most especially my mother, father, brother, and sister, who, if they ever got organized, could tell you a thing or two about me. I don't know how I would have taken to being reduced to a literary caricature, but each of my folks has taken it in stride. If I have thrown my characterizations of my parents off balance by emphasizing their foibles, it is for the simple reason that I find it impossible to make light of their virtues. "My mother and father were compassionate, generous, witty, wise, and loving," makes a most unpromising start to a book of humorous memoirs.

A lot of these pieces were laboriously proofread by family and friends, most especially my brother, Geoff; his wife, Phyllis; and my godfather, Professor Andrew Bongiorno of Oberlin College. So if you come across a misplaced modifier or a superfluous adverb it is entirely their fault.

I also want to thank my friends who suffered with me through the times I describe, and put up with my interrogations at all hours. They are: Hugh and Judy Cuthbertson, Bob Farmer, Deke Harrison, Marnie Farmer, Dan and Ellen Pearlman, Al and Chris Varner, and Rusty Vernet. I would also like to thank my sister, Helen, for her painful recollections of growing up in Greenwich, and Scott Tappan, whose mother's vacuum still rings in his ears, for giving me the idea for the final section of "Lift Your Feet."

You might think that a man who goes on to thank his in-laws will thank anyone, but you don't know my in-laws, Robert and Katherine Huntington, who have unswervingly supported me in my implausible pursuits.

And finally I wish to thank *The Atlantic Monthly,* in which many of these pieces first appeared, and most especially Executive Editor Dick Todd, who also acted as my editor on behalf of the Atlantic Monthly Press. My thanks, also, to my publisher, Peter Davison, for his enthusiasm and support. This book was written under an Atlantic Grant.

I'm afraid that doesn't leave any gratitude for Stacks Supervisor Margaret Holton Minky and her capable staff at the T. Grayson Marbelfoot Memorial Library, but they weren't any help, anyway.

                                        Andrew Ward

New Haven, 1977

Preface to the
1991 Edition

When *Fits & Starts* was first published in 1977, I got a lot of phone calls. But none of them were about my book.

In fact a lot of them were wrong numbers. My phone number was a slippery digit away from the number for Big John's Towing Service, and at all hours of the day or night his customers would call me: stuck in snowbanks, down to their last quarters, fumbling with their frozen mittens at the dials of wind-whipped roadside phones.

I was pretty nice about it at first, but when the phone rang at five o'clock one winter morning and a man bellowed, "Where's your truck, you son of a bitch?" something within me gave way.

"Wait there," I told him. "I'm on my way."

For a while I thought this was pretty damn funny, and

if I'd been a comic instead of a humorist I might have left
well enough alone. But when I tried to get back to sleep I
began to envision the desperate caller stalled somewhere
on the parkway, his family shivering in the shadow of his
upraised hood, awaiting deliverance from Big John's
truck.

So I switched on the light, and I called Big John.

"Listen," I told Big John, backing away from the
whole truth, "I just got a wrong-number call from a guy
who's waiting for one of your trucks, and he sounded
kind of mad."

"Yeah?" said Big John. "Who *is* this?"

"Uh, Mr. Howard Sprinkles," I told him.

"Well, Mr. Sprinkles," Big John said, "will you do
me a favor?"

"I sure will, Big John," I said.

"Will you tell him, Mr. Sprinkles, that I ain't sending
no truck to nobody what don't got the onions to speak
for himself?"

My first lesson in the distinction between humorists and
comedians came in my senior year in high school on something called Compass Night. "Compass" was the name
of the high-school yearbook, which ran a poll to find out
who was best looking, most popular, most athletic, best
dressed, most school spirited, and so on.

By my senior year I was out of the running in every
category but one—class wit—for which I'd been nomi-
nated by my home-room representative. I had already
been described in the class will as having left "a trail of
laughter" wherever I went, so I figured maybe I had a
chance.

My chief rival was an overweight, leering, large-mouthed bass named Beefy Galliano, who, at his most introspective, liked to babble gibberish at foreign-exchange students. The way I saw it, Beefy suffered from an excess of personality, so I decided to spend the weeks of the campaign being especially droll.

But Beefy clobbered me at the polls, burying me in every precinct: college preparatory, distributive education, industrial arts. I didn't understand why until Compass Night, when, to add insult to insult, I was required as a yearbook editor to present Beefy with his award.

I tried to make the best of things by preparing some dryly witty and yet gracious concessionary remarks. But before I could murmur them into the microphone, Beefy grabbed his award, stuffed it into his mouth, and performed a couple of thunderous balletic leaps off into the wings, drowning me out in the ensuing hilarity.

Early on in my career I got billed as a humorist. I hadn't set out to become a humorist, nor, as the final chapter of this book demonstrates, did I try to remain one. I sort of backed into humor, and I've been backing in and out of it ever since.

I hope you'll find these memoirs every bit as premature as they were when they were first published. I was thirty when I wrote *Fits & Starts*, but I think of it as my last act of adolescence. Few of these pieces end happily, so I guess my reminiscences fit the classic comedic mold only if they are recalled with enough composure to imply that in the long run, at least, I came out of my boyhood in one piece.

But my composure didn't last much beyond the publication of my memoirs, and maybe now that another fifteen years have passed I can tell you why.

Fits & Starts was my first book, and it launched me on my very first author's tour, a swashbuckling junket through a gauntlet of Northeastern libraries, clubs, broadcasting studios, bookstores, and retirement centers.

Up to that point being a humorist had been a pretty safe business. The pay was lousy, but with the low pay came low expectations that never extended beyond what I put on paper in the privacy of my own home. But now the Little, Brown publicity department expected me to represent my literary self in person, to personify the voice it took me a hundred rewrites to contrive.

My first stop was a little radio breakfast show hostessed by a caped and imperious old matron who happened to own the station.

She hadn't read my book, and she commanded me to write down ten questions she could ask me about it. "I don't have time to read *every* little thing that comes along," she explained with a grand sweep of her wattled, bangled arm.

"But you know," she said brightly when she got me on the air, "one thing I wondered as I absolutely *devoured* your book last night, Mr. Ward, was . . ." And here she paused, squinting at my hasty scrawl.

I was then asked to speak to an entirely geriatric women's club in Boston, where one lady in the first row actually listened through an earhorn, stopping every now and then to shake her head and declare, "It's impossible. I can't hear him."

After my remarks, the president apologized to me for the low turnout. "But unfortunately, Mr. Ward," she told me, taking me aside, "last year half of our membership died."

My first television appearance was on an afternoon

show hosted by a silver-haired former news anchorman who, holding the book up gingerly to the camera as though it might be an agent of infectious disease, asked me a hard-hitting question about the generation gap.

I must have said something wrong, because he brought the interview to an immediate close by slamming the book down on an endtable and asking if it had ever occurred to me that maybe his generation was just a little too busy surviving the Depression and fighting a world war to wipe my nose for me.

But the show that still enjoys regular syndication in my nightmares was a televised breakfast hour anchored by a tough, Polly Bergen look-alike in black chiffon who barked at her makeup man during commercial breaks. She looked so formidable that I was actually relieved when I got bumped from that morning's broadcast by an expert on biorhythms who sat beside me backstage before his appearance, dashing off random, last-minute charts on shirt cardboards and labeling them with the names of various Red Sox players.

But as I rose to leave I was told that I would be "post-taped" after the show for later broadcast. This meant that the hostess had to change her ensemble, and by the time I was led out onto the set—a tiny wicker salon punctuated with potted ferns—she was feuding again with her makeup man.

"Oo-oo," he suddenly hooted at her during the last seconds of the director's countdown, "I can see up your dre-ess!"

Flustered, anxious, jammed into my little straw chair as the cameras closed in, I let out a small, strangled chuckle.

My hostess whirled around and glared at me for a

moment, then flashed her teeth at the teleprompter on the count of zero. "Today," she read in a pleasant sing-song, "we welcome Andrew Ward who, at the ripe old age of thirty, has written his memoirs.

"Tell me, Mr. Ward," she suddenly sneered, departing from her text, "who do you think is going to read your book *besides your family*?"

It was a good question, but she should have asked you.

Howard Sprinkles
Bainbridge Island, Washington, 1991

Fits and Starts

To
Debbie and Jake

... and now Casey
as well.

U-Turn

I WILL NOT CLAIM that my father made a wrong turn on every trip I took with him when I was a boy in the 1950's. Like everyone else, he had his ups and downs. But even on his best days he could fall prey to his fatally independent nature.

My father despised getting directions, be they oral, written, or diagrammed, and if he followed them at all he followed them selectively, rejecting whatever turns seemed to him unreasonable. "Turn right at Shilk's Liquor Store," the directions might command, and my father would pause at the intersection, regard the flow of traffic, declare, "They can't mean *this* Shilk's Liquor Store," and shoot past to new and uncharted destinations.

This was especially true on trips to places he had visited in the distant past: in his childhood, say, or on his honeymoon. Often he would dispense with directions entirely on these trips, for he seemed to believe that all the regions he had travelled in his youth were mapped out in his memory, or should have been, and all he needed were a few old, familiar landmarks to spark his recollection. That few, if any, of these landmarks (fruit stands, bait shops, elm trees) could have survived the intervening years of depression, war, land boom, and highway expansion never fazed him.

There may have been a faint, leftover frontier ethic involved in all this: a conviction that a man was not a man unless he could find his way by tasting the moss on trees or something. Whatever it was, it was misguided, and misguided us for thousands of unnecessary miles.

On one particular trip we had to pass through Blue Island, Illinois, a rank and sullen burg on the outskirts of Chicago. Blue Island's town hall stood at the intersection of two main roads, and we spent an entire morning passing it from different directions. At first my father claimed that Blue Island had two town halls, but as we grew familiar with the place he had to abandon this thesis. After a third jog past the town hall my father gritted his teeth, took a hard left, and announced, "We're on our way out of here at last." But in a few minutes we passed it again, and it was only by following a caravan of church-chartered buses that we finally got through.

My father had a special hatred for the chatty, stylized, mimeographed maps hostesses sent along with their invitations. He approached these with almost the same degree of suspicion with which he accepted the invitations in the first place. He had less scorn for official maps, though sometimes when we were lost he would stop at a gas station to get a fresh map, as if the one he had been using had gone stale.

It was my mother's function on family outings to sit up front and hold the map, and this she would do, chewing nervously on the inside of her cheek and glancing at the speedometer from time to time (as wrong turn compounded wrong turn, my father tended to step on the gas a little heavily). He made token inquiries of her in her capacity as navigator, but followed her replies with, "Are you damn sure?" or "That can't be right." And when my mother offered to give him Rand McNally verification of her suggestions, he would shake his head with astonishment and exclaim, "How can you expect me to look at the map while I'm driving?"

My mother, recognizing how my father tangled his pride in steering his family to its goals, rarely asserted herself as keeper of the map. When this timidity could be construed as incompetence or dereliction of duty, my father would so construe it, turn to her, and say, "Weren't we supposed to take that road back there?"

"Yes," my mother would reply, thoroughly rattled by this time, "but I thought you knew that."

With a great sigh my father would draw up to the curb, try for a moment to appear to listen to his wife's navigational theories, and finally snatch the map away from her. Then, shoulders hunched, driving glasses raised, he would give the map a cold, skeptical squint, his nose grazing its surface.

The three of us in back — my older brother, my younger sister, and I — would not know to what extent these missed turns and failed landmarks were affecting my father's disposition until he dropped the map, put the car in reverse, and — hat ajar, glasses askew, mouth agape — turned his drained face around to regard the traffic through the rear window. When we saw the desperation in his eyes and heard the quickness of his breaths we knew that what had seemed a laughing matter was now deadly serious business.

My father's father knew very little about cars, but he was nonetheless full of automotive lore, which he could deliver with an impressive sprinkling of technical terms — *magneto, differential,* and *bushing* figuring most prominently. In the late Forties my grandfather took an unaccountable shine to a Hudson dealer named Happy who operated out of a lot near Cleveland, Ohio. As far as Grandpa was concerned, Happy was America's only honest car dealer, and the Hudson (later the Cadillac when Hudson went out of business) was the finest machine on the road. If my grandfather knew little about cars, his son knew less, and was apparently so cowed by Grandpa's overconfident magneto references that even when he was in a position to get whopping breaks on Fords and Lincolns, even when he did not live anywhere near Cleveland, my father bought Hudsons from Happy.

Hudsons were tubby, sloping cars which, parked curbside on a winter day, could be mistaken for forlorn and plow-packed slabs of snow. Their interiors were upholstered in a gray, absorbent fuzz which, after a few weeks' wear, reeked with every odor through which we journeyed: cigarette smoke, gasoline fumes, the sooty effluent of our native Chicago.

I had a tendency to get carsick, an affliction in no way mitigated by the comforts of our Hudsons. Whenever I complained of queasiness my mother suggested that I lie back and stare outside at something stable, like the trees. But by leaning back I not only fell prey to every jounce and sway, but to all the aromas of industry as well, and in no time I would find myself standing by the car on some unfamiliar roadside, trying to determine whether actual vomiting was in the cards.

My father went along with my always inconclusive whoopsy stops (as my sister gleefully called them), but it required everything short of threatening him with physical harm to get him to stop for less pressing purposes. He could drive for five, six hours at a stretch and then stop only because the rest of us could stand it no longer.

His own father would stop for anything — let a passenger casually express a fondness for ice-cream sodas, and my grandfather would jam on the brakes, swerve across lanes of heavy traffic, and deliver his carload to the nearest dairy bar. My father must have resolved, during one of his parents' lurching, distracted tours, that when he grew up and had a car and family of his own, his trips would be run on a strictly no-nonsense basis.

When, at long last, my father was convinced of our aggregate need to stop for food, sleep, and relief, the Law of the Fifth Choice would overtake our deliberations. We never selected the first restaurant we passed once meal time was announced. It was assumed by all that better spots awaited us around the bend, and it's a wonder these first eateries stayed in business. The second restaurant we came to would be either fancier or slummier than the general expectation, and if it was fancier, the third would seem slummier, and vice versa. The fourth restaurant would look fine to all but one of us, whose objections ("They won't have burgers," "They'll require ties") could not be argued down until we were miles past.

A gloomy apprehension set in. Had we passed up our last chance? The miles stretched and multiplied without a sign of an eatery, and we all resolved that no matter what we came to next — Chinese, greasy spoon, barbecue — we would settle for it. Thus, without fail, we obeyed the Law of the Fifth Choice.

Once inside the restaurant (which would usually be nearing closing time) my father would command, "Order first," before we could make it to the rest rooms. He judged the wisdom of our orders not on the basis of price, taste, or nutritional value, but on how long it would take to prepare. Ordering dessert was an act of defiance in our family, and if we lingered over it my father would glare at us, jingling his keys to remind us of our purpose.

No two siblings outside the animal kingdom had as intense a sense of territorial imperative as my sister and I, and some of our fiercest battles were waged over the question of whose portion of the back seat was whose. At one point my parents attempted to settle this dispute by sticking a length of tape down the center of the seat, but there then ensued a battle over whose portion of the tape was whose, which was no improvement. In the end, my brother, who liked to sit up front with the grownups, was deployed to keep us separated. Five years my senior, seven years my sister's senior, my brother seemed at times to regard us as nephew and niece rather than brother and sister, and always tried to avoid any categorical association with us. Seated in our midst he would lean far forward, arms crossed along the backrest of the front seat, trying to engage his parents in sophisticated conversation while my sister and I hurled Cracker Jacks at each other behind his back.

Because of my weak stomach I could not read, draw, or work puzzles on car trips, and had to make do with window games. These consisted of sticking my head out the window and holding it there until the flesh began to freeze, seeing how long I could hold my cupped hand steady in the buffeting highway wind, making harmonicas and soda bottles sound out the window, and, sometimes, spitting out the window, though this was a dangerously suggestive activity for someone with a low nausea threshold. In patriotic moods I held banners of cloth and newspaper in the wind to make them flutter, but this was eventually prohibited after one of my flags got loose, swooped around inside the car, and swirled across my father's field of vision, very nearly forcing him off onto the right road.

A few years ago my father took us to visit an old friend named Bates who was summering on his farm in New Hampshire. Mr. Bates is the kind of man who sorts his screws according to length, gauge, and function in specially saved, labelled, matching jars, and openly advises everyone to follow his example. It is quite possible that Mr. Bates has never taken a wrong turn in his life.

During the course of the visit word leaked out that my father had had some difficulty in finding the Bates homestead. So when we were preparing to leave, Mr. Bates announced that he was going to lead us back to the main highway. My father did his best to talk him out of it, but my father's best was no match for Mr. Bates, who was not going to be responsible for any confusion and dismay on his quiet country lanes. So, declaring that he would stop for gas along the way, and sternly suggesting that my father do the same, Mr. Bates got into his car and led us out the driveway.

All this grated terribly on my father. Reading maps was slavish enough, but nothing compared to following behind his old friend's fender. By the time he reached the gas station, my father had resolved that he was going to lose Mr. Bates.

"Now, for God's sake," he commanded, drawing up to the pump, "nobody go to the bathroom."

As the mechanic finished pumping gas into our car, Mr. Bates ducked into the station to pick up a can of windshield wiper solvent. Seeing his opening, my father paid the mechanic and sped out onto the road.

Dad's determination to escape Mr. Bates and his dictates worked wonders on his sense of direction, and we reached the highway without a hitch, but a few miles down the road my father realized that he had given the mechanic a twenty dollar bill for a five dollar purchase, and pulled the car over to the side of the

road. He wondered for a moment if his escape had
been worth the extra fifteen dollars, but finally, with
a defeated sigh, he turned the car around to pick up his
change.

A mile or so back toward the station, we caught sight
of Bates speeding along in the opposite direction, angrily shouting, "You're going the wrong way!" and
waving my father's change.

When the sky darkened and the shadows lengthened
along the markerless country road, a vehement majority
would regain its voice and bully my now weary and self-
castigating father into submitting to the final humilia-
tion: asking directions of total strangers. These, if we
could not find a gas station attendant, tended to be highway flag-men, school route traffic patrolmen, children,
and great-legged, housecoated women with trowels, few
of whom ever had any idea what we were talking about.

My mother tried to take some of the edge off my
father's anguish by soliciting the guidance herself, leaning out her window and cheerfully beckoning some ap-
prehensive local to our side. The directions we were
given usually went something like this:

"Purling. Purling . . . Can't say as I know of any
Purlings hereabouts." (At this point my father would
race the engine a little, knuckles white along the steering
wheel.) "But I'll tell you what you do. Which way is this
car facing? Oh, yeah. Well, I'd turn around just to start
with and then head straight back over there about two,
seven miles, maybe less — must be four, five traffic
lights at least — until you get to this house set back
from the road a little. It's a white house last time I

looked, although those Brideys — they're the ones who own the place — they're always painting it different colors. Anyway, you bear right down there, I think — only, don't *turn* right. God, don't ever *turn* right there. That won't get you anywhere. *Bear* right, like I said, onto I think it's West Street or Pershing Circle — some name like that — and just keep right on making your turns until you're over in Kerkhoven or Basco and then watch for signs or ask somebody, or something."

My father could barely contain himself during these expositions, and whispered to my mother to thank the man for his help well before he was finished giving us the full benefit of his counsel. Oral directions like these were almost entirely useless to us, of course, because even if they were accurate and we got them straight, my father, as with the mimeographed instructions and the oil company maps, used them selectively.

"He didn't mean *this* Hagensbach railroad station," he'd exclaim, and the self-imposed goose chase would continue.

Sic in Transit

AS FAR BACK AS I can remember, any form of transportation which has denied me access to solid ground has made me sick to my stomach; so it was with mixed emotions, at best, that I received the news from my father that the family was going to move to New Delhi, India. I was only eight at the time, but I knew that between America and India lay vast expanses of water which we would probably have to traverse by boat. I envisioned myself — accurately, as it turned out — heaving over the rails of passenger liners into the raging Atlantic, the wine-dark Mediterranean, the sun-slapped Red and Arabian Seas.

For a time, even as my mother sent off all but our most essential possessions in a tin-encased lift van, I

clung to the thin hope that the family was actually
moving to Indiana. All I had seen of Indiana was the
fumy squalor of Gary (where, in fact, near Dobbie's
Hotel, I had once thrown up on my sister), but I would
have preferred it to the uncertainties of life in a land
half a tipsy, tumbling world away.

I don't remember very much about our voyage to
India, perhaps because I spent most of it under the influ-
ence of Dramamine. "I'm so proud of you, Andy," my
mother told me as I sat drugged and bundled in a deck
chair, gaping at the passing sea. "You're being so well
behaved."

We took the sleek, gigantic S.S. *United States* from
New York to London in February of 1954. The Ford
Foundation, for which my father was about to work as
an educational consultant, booked us in the first-class
section, in the belief — long since abandoned — that the
only way it could lure people to its overseas offices was
to offer them the finest accommodations.

This meant that we had our own steward, a private
bath, a spacious cabin, and elaborate entrées to choose
from in the cavernous, gilded dining room; but it did
not take my brother, my sister, and me long to discover,
amid the minks and blazers, that we were the only children in the first-class section. Sometimes we would try to
converse with the children travelling in cabin class, but
this was frowned upon by our steward. "Come on,
kids," he told us, shooing us back to our stateroom,
"this is the *United States*. We can't have you mixing up
the classes."

From London to Bombay we took a British liner
called the S.S. *Strathmore*. The *Strathmore* was a creak-

ing relic of the old Peninsula and Orient line, which, like the British Raj it had transported, was in a state of resigned and dignified decline. I spent most of my time treading water in the pool, having discovered that this tended to mitigate the effects of the old ship's pitching and rolling, and I only began to realize what a peculiar world we were entering when we docked at Port Said and a magician calling himself the Gully-Gully Man sat down to perform and a succession of doves languidly flapped from his mouth.

But even that proved a tame precursor. The first man to step toward us as we came out of customs in Bombay was a leper with a snuffling gap where his nose had been, and as we made our way toward our taxi, legless men with leather strapped like slippers to their stumps swung about at our feet, snatching at our trousers, shaking cans and bowls, and begging for baksheesh.

Convinced that her children were only a misstep from death's door, my mother did everything she could during our train ride to New Delhi to keep us away from bacteria. We were allowed to eat only bananas — naturally protected by their skins — and every time we touched the seat or the window or, God forbid, the floor with our bare hands as we sped through Gujarat and Rajasthan, she would pounce on us with alcohol and cotton swabs.

The Foundation provided us with a lot of fringe benefits, chief among which was a huge, whitewashed, parabolic house on the outskirts of New Delhi. It was surrounded by lawns, flower beds, ornamental hedges, and fruit trees, and as we approached it through white gates on a red quartz gravel drive, my sister, who had been nearly persuaded by her brothers that we were going to be living in a mud hut, lifted her doll to the window and said, "See, Bertha? I told you we were moving to a palace."

A palace it was, if only because of the servants. As we stepped into the clean, gleaming house, seven of them hurried toward us, bare feet slapping softly on the stone floor, and pulled our bags from our hands, our coats from our backs, our hats from our heads, and darted off into the house, leaving us dazed and fidgety in the hall. From that day forward for a total of four years, whenever any of us tried to do something for ourselves — carry a book upstairs, make our beds, fetch a glass of water from the refrigerator — someone, usually Sriram, our bearer, would dash in from his vigil in the verandah and head us off. "Permit me," he would mutter irritably, unmaking our beds and laying the sheets over the footboard to air them out or snatching a glass away and serving it properly, complete with ice, lime wedge, swizzle stick, coaster, and napkin. We children adapted pretty quickly to all this service, but it troubled my parents deeply, and they were always trying to sneak things past the staff and reminding us to say "Thank you" whenever we were served, so that "thank you's" interrupted our conversation like hiccups.

My parents were liberal and academic and decided right away to immerse their children in the culture by enrolling us in an Indian school. Actually, it turned out to be an Anglo-Indian school called Miss Enid's Academy for Young Masters and Misses. Miss Enid was a towering, sunburned woman with pale red hair. She wore saris and a man's wristwatch, and shod her white, spreading feet in gold plastic sandals. "Come along, Andrew," she said, leading me to my new class. "We must not fall behind, must we?"

When I'd left Chicago, my third-grade classmates were just getting around to tackling numerals and poster-painting bunnies, and it didn't take long to establish that I was already miles behind my new classmates at Miss Enid's — that is, it didn't take long once I had established who my classmates were. The school was divided into forms, and though I still don't know what forms are, I do know they aren't the same as grades, since every time I tried to sit in the third form I was sternly directed elsewhere.

My classmates turned out to be half as tall as I and twice as smart. One boy, a multilingual Dane named Erik, could even use a slide rule, and would sit next to me at the table on Miss Enid's verandah, clicking and calculating as I wistfully drew bunnies in my composition book.

Miss Enid attributed my problems with mathematics, English — the whole catastrophe — to shyness. "He will *blossom* under our tutelage," she assured my mother. "It is simply a matter of confidence." But even she lost confidence after a few weeks, and set me up with one of her assistants in a special tent on the front lawn. The assistant's name was Miss Pai, and she was beautiful. Miss Enid made saris look like laundry hung out to dry, but on Miss Pai they looked like flowers which had spontaneously wrapped themselves around her. She was kind, too, and may even have been a good teacher; I don't know. When she tried to teach me my multiplication tables, I couldn't take my eyes off her bare midriff, and we never got anywhere.

After a couple of months at Miss Enid's I contracted encephalitis. The disease had been making the rounds that spring, and several children in Delhi had died from it. All I remember is coming home from school with a burning sensation under my skull, losing consciousness as our bearer carried me up the stairs, and then bobbing up out of a coma to have my spine tapped and my forehead iced. A prayer vigil was set up in our downstairs verandah by Hindu, Moslem, Buddhist, and Christian servants, and last-resort, experimental drugs were flown in from New York. One way or another I recovered, but the disease scared the hell out of my parents, and they enrolled me and my sister in The American School, which was housed in the barracks of a defunct downtown hotel and run by local American memsahibs.

As soon as I set foot in The American School I felt at home. "Get some clay, Andy," the teacher said. "We're all going to make hand-print ash trays for our mummies and daddies."

The staff did everything it could to make the school as American as possible, and every morning Miss Vinkataraman, our Madrasi teacher, would lead us in The Lord's Prayer and The Pledge of Allegiance. Through the school our family came into contact with a sizable American community, complete with barbecues, softball games, and fireworks on the Fourth of July.

There were only eight of us in the third grade, and all the boys were Cub Scouts, so I joined up right away. A dhursee was hired to sew me a uniform, we sent back to the States for a cap and a manual, and every Saturday I met with my friends to learn about knots, whittling, bicycle safety. Our den mother was an ex-WAC named Mrs. Barry, who began each meeting by saying, "What I'm going to teach you this morning could save your life someday, so listen up."

I listened up, but I never could figure how that could apply to flag folding, lanyard braiding, candle dipping, and a lot of the other minor crafts she taught us. It was also difficult to get a sense of urgency when, at snack time, cookies and Coca-Cola were served to us by Mrs. Barry's stooped, white-coated bearer, who, when I once dropped my napkin on the lawn, dove to the ground to retrieve it for me.

My brother was too old for The American School, so he was tutored at home by an Indian, and his best friends were our driver, and the Sikh youth who delivered eggs to the house. India fascinated him, but it mattered to my sister and me only insofar as lizards clung to the walls, snakes slipped through the garden, jackals howled outside the compound at night, and grown men were deferential in our paths. I suppose it sounds as though it should have mattered a great deal, but it didn't; I spent my time playing baseball and cowboys and Indians, and, at school, learning the Gettysburg Address and eating peanut butter sandwiches from Looney Tunes lunch boxes.

Part of the package the Ford Foundation offered its personnel was a biannual, expenses-paid home leave. As a consequence, our family wound up circling the globe three times. You might think that in all that time we might have mastered the art of travelling light. But we never did. We were all to blame for this — my father had to have his files, my brother had to have his books, my sister had to have her dolls, I had to have a full battalion of lead soldiers with me at all times — but a great deal of our luggage consisted of my mother's paraphernalia. There was always a battle over who was going to have to carry her toiletry cases; they had faulty handles, weighed as much as bowling balls, and made ominous, muffled clinking noises in transit.

On some trips we travelled with as many as twenty-four pieces of luggage, which, in cities where the porters were striking, we would sometimes have to carry ourselves. This we accomplished in intricate shifts, picking up half the bags and carrying them a little distance, stationing my sister by them, dashing back for the rest and carrying them past the first batch, moving my sister up to the second batch as we dashed back for the first, and in this fashion leapfrogging our way through the cities of Europe, the Middle East, and Asia.

Not all this luggage came in the form of suitcases or garment bags — a lot of it consisted of cardboard department-store boxes tied up with string — but of course all of it had to be accounted for, and my father spent a lot of his middle years standing by doormen, runways, docks, and railroad tracks totalling up the baggage.

"Dewy," he'd sometimes exclaim as our flight was announced or our taxi pulled away, leaving him amid the luggage on the curb, "I only count twenty-two pieces!"

"But that's all there were, dear," my mother told him.

"No, there are supposed to be twenty-four!"

"Oh my god. Are you sure?"

"Of course I'm sure!" my father barked, which was his way of expressing himself in moments of extreme doubt.

So the whole family would wade in and take up the count, each of us tabulating at the top of his voice and trying to shush the others, each neglecting to figure in the bag or two he was holding, each arriving at a different total, until my brother and I were yelling at each other, my sister (convinced that her dolls' suitcases were among the missing pieces) was in tears, my mother was wild-eyed, and my father, who had stood back with a disgusted smirk as his family babbled through the baggage, stepped forward.

"All right, for god's sake, settle down!" he commanded. "I'm going to count once more, and this is going to be it."

So, as we all stood by in angry, resentful silence, he would tally up the luggage again.

". . . twenty, twenty-one, and my camera makes twenty-two. There we are. Twenty-two pieces. Nothing to get excited about. It's all here."

My father could be unsettling company on our family's trips. He hated above all things to be cooped up and to operate on somebody else's timetable, which made him something of a menace in restaurants. That restaurants required him to *pay* for his imprisonment made him furious, and around the soup course, if not sooner, he would get this choked look and either descend into a twitchy silence, glancing around as if afraid he were about to be ambushed, or correct his children's manners and hurry us through our meal. He developed a suspicion that all waiters were out to cheat him, and often caused a scene when the check was brought, leaning into the candlelight to examine and reexamine the addition, sometimes even calling for the menu to check the pricing, as his family shrunk out of the establishment to wait on the street.

"I got him," he once declared triumphantly, cheered by the confirmation of his worst suspicions. "He had us down for an extra salad!"

On my family's travels I developed my own special areas of expertise. I could have taught a course in Comparative Club Sandwiches — Hong Kong's Peninsula Hotel had the finest by far — but my major field was air-sick bags.

Air-sick bags varied considerably from airline to airline. BOAC barely deigned to provide them, and what they supplied were simply miniaturized grocery bags. To this day the slightest whiff of a brown paper bag is enough to send me reeling. Pan American had the best air bags — plastic-lined and capacious with all sorts of soothing phrases printed on them in five languages — and Indian Airlines had the worst. The bag I was given aboard one I.A. flight into Kashmir wasn't a bag at all but a cardboard tube plugged at one end with a cardboard disc which, under the pressure I miserably applied to it somewhere over Jammu, suddenly gave way.

That particular flight was eventful in many ways. The plane was a shuddering DC2, and our fellow-passengers were for the most part Kashmiri shepherds returning from a government-sponsored agricultural fair. One shepherd across the aisle from me had a bound goose in his lap which, when we hit heavy weather, got one wing loose and flapped the length of the cabin, honking like a Model T, until it was at last hugged to the aisle floor and returned to its owner. As we neared the high peaks surrounding the Vale of Kashmir, our captain's voice came crackling over the loudspeaker, requesting that all passengers please gather in the rear of the cabin so as to assist him in tipping the nose of the craft sufficiently to clear an impending mountain. My mother gave out a small, strangled noise and herded her children back and stood with us, holding our hands in a cold, tight grip. "Oh kids," she exclaimed, her voice and eyebrows high as we neared the obstructing peak, "isn't this fun?"

Our itineraries hopped us through the world in fits and starts as my father caught this or that meeting in this or that capital, so that travelling became something like twirling the dial on a television set; we never quite knew what was going to show up outside our porthole. One day I found myself pedal-boating on Lake Lugano; another day I stood with my father in the lobby of a hotel in Saigon, listening as the manager instructed him on how to walk through the city without getting stoned to death. The following day I tramped through the throttled ruins of Angkor Wat, trying to keep the ever-present man-eating ants from accumulating on my shoes. Christmas I stood in the shepherds' field outside Bethlehem, watching the sun descend; New Year's I marched along the battlements of Windsor.

It was all heady stuff, and it was at the Hotel St.

George in Beirut, on our final trip to America, that my father decided he had made the right choice in accepting a stateside job. "I'm going to keep it simple tonight," he overheard my sister tell me as the two of us headed down to the dining room. "Snails and peach melba."

On those mornings when we had to catch a plane, my parents always arose a half-hour or so before their children. "It's not time," my mother would tell us when we stirred after the clinky chatter of the travel alarm. "Go back to sleep."

So the three of us would pretend to doze off again in our stiff, clean hotel sheets as my parents made their way through the room, tenderly packing our clothes, books, and toys. Even now, when my bed is jostled as my wife gets up for work or my small son pads in to ask to be dressed, I sometimes slip back to those dark and peaceable hours of morning when my parents reached under our beds to retrieve a stray sock, a doll's slipper, a tin soldier, and paused over us to speak their children's names in whispers.

Jingle Shoes

MY FAMILY MOVED back to the States barely a month after my thirteenth birthday. We had selected our new house in Riverside, Connecticut, while we were still in India. My father had taken a whirlwind globe-circling trip to America to search for a new home among the suburbs of New York, and returned to New Delhi with slides of houses in Riverside. His pictures made the place look as wholesome and American as Hannibal, Missouri. Barefoot boys fished from rowboats on a dark, logy river, willows wept along twisting country lanes, clapboard houses shimmered amid lush, green lawns. The house we settled on looked capacious and welcoming in my father's slides, but as it turned out he must have used a wide-angle lens and some special fil-

ters, because when we actually got to the house it looked
about as spacious as a caboose.

The house was split-level, a format we never did get
used to. We were always forgetting how short the stair-
cases were and stepping uselessly into the air above the
top landing on our way up and colliding with the bottom
landing on our way down. Living in the house was like
living in a halved club sandwich. The ceilings were low,
the windows few, and for the seven years we lived there
claustrophobia would exacerbate the desperation with
which our family approached its crises.

Our house was part of Capezzio Hills, a development
on a bank of the Mianus River. Mr. Capezzio himself
lived a few doors down in a huge house on an artificial
hill, which gave everyone else in the neighborhood a
subordinate feeling. Possessive and compulsive, he never
quite let go of the properties he sold, and used to patrol
the development during his off hours, picking up pop-
sicle wrappers, moving tricycles out of driveways, and
occasionally ringing doorbells to suggest plantings, tree
prunings, hedge trimmings along Capezzio Boulevard,
the development's main thoroughfare.

"Look," he once said, ducking into our house as we
were sitting down to dinner, "it's too bare out there.
You need tomatoes. Some nice pomodoro plantings."

My father, misunderstanding Capezzio's implicit
command, replied that we would love some tomatoes,
and he was awfully nice to offer us some.

Capezzio frowned, marched out of the house, and
later returned in a sour mood with three tomato seedlings in a brown paper bag.

"All right, here they are. Supersonic seedlings and
they don't come any better," he grumbled, handing the

bag to my father. "But this is it. You're not getting any more out of me." He led Dad over to a patch of lawn in the middle of the backyard and stood over him in the dying light as my father tentatively spooned — we couldn't find the trowel — the little plants into place.

"O.K.," Mr. Capezzio said, "they're in. Take care of them and they'll take care of you."

But the seedlings did poorly for some reason — maybe the same reason the lawn kept dying on us — and after a few days Mr. Capezzio began to show up with special dusts and sprays and pruning tips to try to buck them up. The plants obviously weighed on my father's mind; every evening when he returned he would head straight for them in his hat and business suit, sometimes with his briefcase still in one hand, and kneel down and chin-chuck the yellowing leaves and re-tie the limp trunks to garden stakes.

Tomatoes finally showed up on them, but before they ripened, slugs moved in. "That's it, then," Mr. Capezzio said, scowling at my father and jerking the little plants out of the ground. "I don't know how you could have allowed this to happen. You get slugs, and as far as I'm concerned you're all washed up."

My parents' social introduction to Capezzio Hills was no more promising. A lot of the neighbors would only talk about how they were going to move out and get a house with four acres in back country Greenwich. "We'd shingle, but what's the point?" Mrs. Prosciutto, our next-door neighbor, told my mother once. "As soon as Angelo's promo comes through we're getting out of this kind of place."

A welcoming party was thrown for my parents by a

jolly man named Atherton, and at first my mother was touched by the gesture. "What a friendly town," she said, walking out the door.

But it turned out that Atherton threw a party every week. Soon after my parents arrived, a toreadored woman showed up with a Florida tan and exclaimed, "Why, if I were any darker you wouldn't want me in your house!" There was a lot of drinking, and late in the evening my mother was pinched by a cub executive in pop-up toasters, and my father took her home.

From then on my parents kept to themselves. Once, when a neighborhood boy I had been playing with suggested to his father that they invite my parents to join them for a barbecue, the father glared at me and said, "Oh, they won't want to join *us*, son. Didn't you know? *Andy's* parents are *intellectuals*."

I got off to just as rocky a start at Eastern Junior High. My shoes had given out en route from India, and my mother took me to a Beirut clothing store to buy me a new pair. I was glad to be rid of my Indian shoes — they were orange rubber and perforated, and I had been worrying ever since leaving New Delhi that they wouldn't go over well with my new classmates in Riverside — but I wound up buying a pair that were at least as bad. They were brown suede with crepe soles and large, square buckles that jingled slightly when I walked. The Lebanese salesman insisted they were all the rage in America, and I believed him.

"You will be seeing," he called after me as I jingled out the door. "You will be the latest thing."

The Riverside teenager of the early 1960's adhered

to a strict dress code. Much has been written about what girls had to wear at the time — Villager blouses, kilt-pinned pleated skirts, Capezio flats — but boys' wear was no less circumscribed. If you intended to get any-where in life, you wore a crewneck sweater (weather permitting), a white or light blue button-down shirt with the sleeves rolled up two turns, khaki pants with cuffs, a plain black belt (if your pants didn't have sewn-in hitching buckles), white socks (black socks after six), and brown penny loafers. Permissible variations were letter sweaters (white cardigan with the letter sewn over the right pocket, unless you got the letter in an obscure, loner sport like cross-country running, in which case nobody cared what you wore) or, if you were an officer of the student council, a tie (thin and sub-dued) and a sports jacket (preferably madras or cor-duroy).

None of this was written down anywhere, but it might as well have been. Industrial Arts majors tended toward shiny shirts, black Levi's, studded belts, and sinister, pointy-toed slip-ons, but only girls with com-municable diseases would go out with them. And there were a few oblivious types who would sneak a pair of oxfords into the formula, or a flannel shirt buttoned up to the throat, but they were audiovisual crewmen or Oceanography Club cadets, and though they might be liked, they would never be well liked.

It was into this latter category that I inadvertently placed myself when I stood to be introduced by Miss Dunky to my new seventh-grade classmates. I wore a lumberjack shirt, green corduroys, a Navajo beaded belt, argyle socks, and, of course, my jingle shoes. I was

undergoing one of my frequent growth spurts at the
time (I grew the most during anxious periods, like
Pinocchio's nose) and none of my clothes fit me. But
even if they had I still would have given the impression
that I had been dressed out of a cardboard box in a
home for backward children.

I'd like to be able to say that none of this mattered to
me, that I just went my own way and to hell with everyone. But it mattered terribly. When I got home each
afternoon I would stomp around the house in a Tinker
Bell fury, threatening to set fire to my wardrobe. "Oh,
now," my mother said, "it doesn't matter what you
wear. Besides, I can hardly hear your shoes at all."

Eventually I worked my way out of my antiquated
wardrobe by sanding away at my jingle shoes until the
soles gave out, tearing holes in my corduroys and blam-
ing them on the clothes drier, spilling paint on my lumberjack shirts in art class. After a dozen trips to the
local sports shops I managed to accumulate all the required elements of an Eastern Junior High School
wardrobe. Though my social life never did recover from
my jingle shoes, at least I could begin to make my own
way.

My sister didn't get off so easy. Her first day as a fifth
grader at the Mianus School she threw up, and, refusing
her teacher's offer of a change of clothes, persuaded the
nurse to let her go home. Like everyone else in the
family, she was a late bloomer. In Riverside, girls were
expected to get most of their blooming out of the way by
twelve, or fake it.

Helen wouldn't fake it, at least not at first, and railed

against the feminine arts as they were prematurely practiced at the Mianus School and then at Eastern Junior
High. Once, in dancing class, a boy had signed himself
up to dance with her: this after weeks during which she
had been reduced to fox-trotting with the instructor.
When, at lunch, her friends were comparing dance
cards, Helen hesitantly mentioned that the boy, Bobby
Barnstable, had reserved a dance. "Oh, Helen," her best
friend told her at the top of her voice. "Don't kid yourself."

"It's sickening!" Helen used to exclaim at the dinner
table. "Everything is boys, boys, boys!"

"Now, dear," my mother told her, "you just give
them a chance to see what a nice, pleasant girl you really
are."

But Helen approached her peers defiantly pony-tailed,
ankle-socked, and jumpered, until at last she came under
the sway of puberty and a ferocious classmate named
Patsy Farrar. It was Patsy Farrar who first introduced
her to the uses of a Bloomingdale's charge card, and
who convinced her to get a Pixie Perm, just like hers.
Helen did everything with a vengeance (as the youngest
child and only daughter she was convinced that she always got the short end of the stick) and in time, along
with half a dozen other girls, came to look exactly like
Patsy Farrar.

"There," Patsy would tell her in the aisle at Bloomingdale's, selecting a handbag that precisely matched her
own, "now you look a hundred times better."

I suppose every teenager thought his family was con-
spicuous, but sometimes it seemed to me that our family

went out of its way to attract attention. As soon as we
moved in, my father made a deal on a scuffed, gray-green
Hudson. It had belonged to a freewheeling Ohio handy-
man who called himself Mr. Screwball and had painted
his logo (a cross-eyed, tongue-lolling face) and slogans
("Have a Happy!" "A nut with ALL THE FIXIN's!") all
over the car. The dealer had repainted it, but in certain
lights the logos and slogans were distinctly visible, and
every afternoon when my mother came to pick me up
among the sleek, shining Fords, Chevies, and Pontiacs
of my friends' parents, I would sneak my way toward
her, walking past the car, through the parking lot, over
the wall that surrounded the school, and then, when I
thought no one was watching, darting back and climbing
in and sitting low in the passenger's seat until we were
safely out of sight.

Rub-Out

They are like grass which groweth up.
In the morning it flourisheth, and groweth up;
in the evening it is cut down, and withereth.
                                    Psalm XC

I USED TO THINK it was my poetic nature that dizzied
me when I smelled the aroma of new-mown grass, but
now I realize it is just a legacy of my boyhood days
behind my family's power mower. It was a discount-
house mower which had been purchased quickly, without
research, in one of those let's-just-go-get-one spasms of
buying that afflicted my parents whenever it came time
to acquire a major appliance.

It was something of an improvement over our old
powerless mower whose clanging blades, when you
pushed too slowly, yanked up the grass by its roots. But
our new mower's motor was something of an after-
thought. The machine tended to stall in grass standing
any higher than three inches. It gave off, when it was

working, a great blue cloud of smoke, a choking stench of oil and gas, and in its wake the clumps of cut grass would smolder on the surface of the lawn like dying cigarettes.

We had about half an acre of grass, front and back, and for whatever reason — lack of shade, topsoil, drainage, or motivation — it died on us around August of every year. Its sickliness triggered a resolute mechanism in my mother's nature. Whenever one of us gently hinted at the long range hopelessness of the situation, she would get this abstracted look, as if God were speaking to her, drowning out our voices.

Her Gospel consisted of the little pamphlets which came packed in bags of lawn care products. Their step-by-step illustrations promised her that all could never be lost, that after every defeat there would be a new, constructive step to take, all the way to the end. Sacks of *Turf Fortifier, Halts, Rid, Scat, Shoo, Scoot,* and *Scram* were piled in our garage from early spring to late fall, awaiting their cues.

"What good is *that* going to do?" I'd ask as she ripped open a bag of something new for me to spread.

"This is going to extend our tillers," she would cheerfully reply, "and fortify our rhizomes."

Whatever it was might have done just that, but it never did our lawn any good. I think our lawn depended so heavily on crab grass, dandelions, even chinch bugs and snow mold for its special hue that once all the herbicides and insecticides had done their work there was nothing left.

I try not to think about the birds and burrowing rodents we must have poisoned during our seven-year

yard war in Riverside, Connecticut. There was one
chemical so lethal that the pamphlet warned us to keep
dogs away until the rain had washed it down, lest it eat
into their paws and up into their brains. Heavily booted,
we took turns watching for dogs over a three-day dry
spell. When it finally did rain, our lawn could be heard
actually to fizz, like a vast spill of soda.

My parents had hoped that the lawn would provide
me with a much needed lesson in the nature of work, and
they were right; it did: especially the numbing, dead-end
side of it. One spring morning I was out spreading something called *Turf Fortifier,* a fertilizer in which I placed
no faith whatsoever. Spreading the stuff seemed to me
wasted motion, so I decided to speed up the job by skipping every other lane. Of course, I had to dispose of
enough of it to convince my parents that I had done a
thorough job, so I set the flow switch on the spreader to
"Full Open" and managed, after a few perfunctory
passes across the yard, to get rid of most of it.

I spent the rest of the day as I pleased, but by the
middle of the following week my secret ploy had gone
public. My uneven and disproportionate dose of *Turf
Fortifier* had raised narrow, crisscrossed lanes of lush
greenery which were detectable, a monument to my
deceit, for the rest of the summer.

The ultimate lawn care product was *Rub-Out,* a slick
and sickly-green powder which, the pamphlet promised,
turned terminal lawns into hearty mulch: the perfect
base upon which to build a new and lasting lawn. So my
mother bought a few bags and assigned me to put our
lawn out of its misery.

I was so terrified that *Rub-Out* could turn me, too,

into a hearty mulch (it looked to me like the green sugar with which Captain Hook had tried to poison Peter Pan) that I did a little dance as I spread it, lifting a foot every few steps to shake the stuff from my shoes. The lawn we sowed afterwards was no healthier than the first, and I wound up spreading *Rub-Out* on an annual basis. We had, in fact, so much hearty mulch under our yard that it became springy, even in death, like a carpet of air filter, and sucked down water like a drain.

I think our family hit bottom the summer my mother decided we were going to have to tear up our dying lawn, spread new topsoil, and start all over.

"We'll be done in a shake," she said. It was one of her favorite phrases, and there was no arguing with her. I had thought until then that she and my father had simply caught the bug which was afflicting everyone in Riverside at the time. But my mother's new project would put us all in a different league. No one in the entire Tristate Metropolitan Area did what we did.

My mother bought special rakes from the hardware store. They came wrapped in a piece of cardboard that had a picture of a sweatless man in casual knits happily tearing up his strangely green and thriving lawn. The idea, my mother told us as we each unwrapped our rakes, was to chop into the turf and jerk it back, ripping the grass up in tidy strips. I always liked to get new tools, and I had to admit that there was something appealing about starting all over. My mother hoped, too, I think, that by pitching in together we would draw closer as a family, exchange life philosophies, fortify our characters along with our tillers and rhizomes.

So we started along the driveway — my parents, my brother, my sister, and I — chopping and ripping. There was some cheerful banter exchanged at first, and sometimes I would catch my mother watching us with pioneer pride shining in her eyes as we worked the suburban earth. In some places along the outer rim of the yard the grass rolled off like lanes of carpet. But more and more we began to hit places where the grass could only be dragged up if we got down on our knees and tore at it with our fingers.

One by one, we began to look back at the remaining expanse of expired grass, and feel something give way within us. The job would clearly be no "shake," what with tearing and prying up the tufts of grass with rakes, shovels, and fingers, and hauling it away in wheelbarrows and wire-handled bushel baskets.

Every now and then, toward the close of the first day, as it began to dawn on us what we were in for, one of us would come up with an idea. Why not burn the lawn away? it was asked. Why not lay artificial turf, a sure-fire money-saver in the long run, whatever the initial expense? How about pachysandra, myrtle, and other hardy ground covers?

But my mother would simply shake her head and bow closer to the ground, and my father, who had accepted this project as one of life's tests of his mettle, would say, "Come on. Let's do it right."

As the days dragged on we all made our own peculiar adjustments to the task at hand. My father, fearing sunstroke, kept an umbrella handy to shade him if he were suddenly overcome. My mother kept a towel beneath her to keep the doomed grass from staining the knees of her pedal-pushers. And their children took to working from low beach chairs, watching TV from a set perched on the sill of an upstairs window.

For two solid weeks we crawled backward in a swirl of dust, snatching at the grass like locusts. People in cars began to come down our dead-end lane and pause in the turnaround to watch us carve a desert out of the nation. I don't know what fears they entertained, but they would have been justified in suspecting that crafty blockbusters had sold the property to a family of sun-crazed and unreconstructed potato farmers. Neighbors who had at first rooted for us, martinis upraised on their patios, took to hurrying past us with anxious, nodding smiles and watching us from indoors, as if our condition were viral.

By the time the old grass was gone, piled in snarled heaps in the wooded lot beside us, the yard had, to our eyes, a pleasing uniformity. We debated keeping it that way, or spreading marble chips, but it was pointed out that there was no guarantee that weeds, even grass, wouldn't start sprouting again, no matter what we did.

So a mountain of dirt was ordered, and dumped in our yard by a baffled man who kept asking us what we were going to do with it, as if he were handing explosives to lunatic children. I think my mother had hoped for crumbled clods of dark loam, but the dirt proved stony and had to be refined by shovelling it through a tipsy screen. After a rain the mountain hardened like cement, and we never did manage to spread all of it; there is still a hump in the yard where the dirt was dumped. During the week it took to spread the soil one or two of us would fall into a rebellious frenzy and stomp off into the house to pace and nap, but we would be shamed back, always, by a look at our mother still laboring in the sun, huddled over the ground as if searching for roots in a famine. And, sometimes, one of us would get stuck, and continue to work even after everyone else had gone inside, even as the sun went down and it was time for dinner, until someone was sent to snap him out of it.

When the yard was finally covered with topsoil, my mother told us it had to be aerated, which meant pushing a toothy, rented machine over it that left little tubular clods all over the place. A rainy period set in, so that the seeds we sowed were washed into bunches which we would have to rake into position until their filamentous roots took hold.

By then our family, normally talkative and gregarious unto itself, had grown sullen and distrustful. As a vague haze of green spread across the yard, we went our separate ways. I found myself drawn to the woods, where I would sit for long periods, observing indigenous vegetation. My father returned to work, my brother to college, my sister to her interchangeable friends.

And the yard, too, stayed true to itself. Within weeks it was weed-ridden, patchy, and dying again. Crab grass, we learned, no less than chinch bugs, and snow mold, and dandelions, thrives in fresh new topsoil.

In the end we did the only decent thing and moved. Our new home had a grand slope of lawn which had thrived, unassisted, since the middle of the nineteenth century. My father would sometimes toe it with his shoes on the way home from the station, but we treated it respectfully, afraid to touch it, lest we trigger some disastrous ecological chain of events for which *Rub-Out* would be the last resort. It was this lawn's salvation, I think, that my mother developed other interests.

I still drive by the old house sometimes. A German couple moved in after us, and raised an impressive chain link fence in the back for their guard dogs, but whatever they tried on the lawn — commands, maybe, and threats — didn't help it any. They were followed by a Japanese couple who I hoped would coax golf green grass up from the poisoned ground with lovely wooden implements and reverent, time-honored techniques, but they had no success at all and soon moved away. Now the onion grass has sprouted up from the matted clutches of crab grass, chinch bugs munch on the last blades of Kentucky Blue, and the snow mold has spread everywhere, unopposed. I don't know who lives there now, but whoever it is has been wise enough to let the damn thing go.

The Naked Man

DOWN THE STREET from us in Riverside lived an elderly couple named Jasper. Mr. Jasper was a retired panelling and flush-door executive who spent most of his time browsing through hardware stores, picking up hose couplings and balls of twine not so much out of immediate need as in its anticipation.

"You can't have enough of this stuff," he'd declare at the register, purchasing a jar of horse glue, a bag of stove bolts.

"Got a million uses, all right," the hardware man would reply encouragingly.

We never saw much of Mrs. Jasper. She was sickly, and rarely left the house. I remember her mostly as a dim, leaning figure in a blue housecoat, hazy through the front door screen as she bayed last minute commands to her retreating husband.

"And don't forget the ointment," we would hear her cry as Mr. Jasper backed out the driveway.

No one seemed to know what ailed Mrs. Jasper. "A bad case of nerves," my mother used to say, and it did seem that whatever was wrong with her had the effect of making her anxious. She was one of those eruptive women around whom whole nations tiptoe. To her credit, she had done everything in her power to evade the vicissitudes of human affairs, venturing out only to sit blanketed on her rear terrace, downing chocolate cherries and watching the river flow.

It was during one of these vigils, on a warm summer's day, that a naked man in a Disney mask drifted by Mrs. Jasper in an aluminum rowboat. The current brought him into view for only a moment, but it gave him time to manage a nod and a wave before he disappeared behind some overhanging foliage.

Flinging her chocolates into the air, Mrs. Jasper burst out of her blanket and rushed shrieking for the phone. Within minutes, a great many police arrived, sirens whooping, and slipped down the riverbank in their shiny shoes to poke along the water's edge. The neighborhood gathered around the house and watched as policemen scanned the far side of the river with binoculars and beat at the underbrush with their nightsticks.

No naked men were spotted, but an indignant bass fisherman was bullhorned ashore and questioned. I suppose the police had hoped he was a quick change artist, but his rowboat turned out to be wooden, and it developed that he was a member of the Board of Estimate and Taxation, which, in Greenwich Township, is something akin to the ministry. Under questioning, the fisherman insisted that he had been alone on the river all morning, that had another man, most especially a naked one, drifted by he would have seen him. Despite his advancing years, the fisherman declared, he had impeccable eyesight, and at his last checkup was pronounced sound as a dollar.

Mrs. Jasper, mistaking the questioning for an arrest, called down from her upstairs window that the fisherman didn't look at all like the man she had seen, that the culprit had been older and heavier.

In a jowly rage, the fisherman raised his hands to the buttons of his shirt, shouting, "I could disrobe, madam, if you want to make sure!"

Embarrassed, the police led him back to his boat and helped him shove off, muddying their trousers. "I tell you," he bellowed as he rowed away, "there's been no nudity!"

After assuring Mrs. Jasper that the whole matter would be the subject of a thorough and ongoing investigation, the police wiped the mud and scattered chocolate cherries off their shoes and departed.

In response to the sighting, mothers started supervised indoor play groups while their husbands took turns patrolling the woods. Locks were changed and alarm systems installed in that disproportionate thrill of fear that sweeps the suburbs at the briefest evincement of the sinister.

Still, I think no one was as haunted by the naked man

as I. He drifted through my dreams for weeks, waving, grinning, dimly familiar. At the time, I was going through a period of extreme highs and lows. On the one hand I fancied myself religious and erected altars in my cellar bedroom late at night, complete with candles and homemade crucifix, before which I knelt, uttering prayers of my own composition.

On the other hand I was libidinous, and had accumulated a storehouse of men's magazines and paperbacks (mostly plantation epics) with the good parts marked off. And when the good parts weren't good enough, I would write my own no-holds-barred versions on legal pads, stacking them in the gaps in the acoustical-tiled ceiling of my room.

I purged myself of such stuff at least a dozen times, pledging with each disposal that it would be my last, but I must have been caught up in some sort of glandular cycle beyond my control, for within weeks I would be at it again, smuggling home airbrushed copies of *Gent* and *Nugget* in my shirt and poring over them as the family slept in the house above me.

I usually disposed of my collections by stuffing them into shopping bags and throwing them out with the trash. But early one spring I decided to purge myself a little more dramatically by dispatching my shame to the bottom of the river. On a cloudy, windy afternoon I lashed a stone to my little heap of magazines and, with a curse, hurled it out over the water. There was an impressive splash, but the stone came loose on contact and left my vile bundle bobbing on the surface, heading for sea. I searched in vain for a stick or a boat with which to retrieve it from the frigid water, imagining an outing of nuns chancing upon it downriver, or the Coast Guard tracing it, with advanced detection techniques, back to me, my mother's boy, my father's son. It began to rain, and I sank to my knees in despair, but when my eyes focused again on the retreating heap I made out a small, dark shape closing in on it. It was my dog, which had followed me from the house. To her, this was all just another game of fetch; she snatched the bundle in her teeth and, coughing away at the water that lapped between her long, dachshund's jaws, hauled it ashore. I jubilantly took the bundle from her, secured another stone to it, and, restraining the dog, hurled it back into the river, where it sank unhesitatingly to the bottom.

I thought then that my sins were safe until that summer, when Mrs. Jasper saw the naked man. Since no trace of him had been found — he seemed to have dematerialized — I developed an unutterable terror that he had risen from the murk of the river itself, constructed of the decayed pages of my drowned shame, a grinning, dripping, monster of smut.

For days after the sighting police patrolled the river disguised as fishermen. Sometimes I would sneak down and watch them from the underbrush, feeling the hair rise on my neck whenever they casually cast their lures over my dumping site. But they never spotted me, or the naked man, perhaps because they soon lost track of their purpose on the river. I remember two of them climbed into their car one evening with a five-pound bass, and soon afterward their vigil was officially terminated.

To calm his wife, Mr. Jasper stuck close to home, pacing his yard and muttering. People were obliquely disappointed that the naked man hadn't reappeared to justify their initial panic and began to speculate that maybe the fisherman had been right; maybe there never had been a naked man; maybe Mrs. Jasper's hives, or piles, or bad feet, or whatever ailed her, made her see things. The play groups started to fall apart, fathers abandoned their forest patrols.

Mr. Jasper resented inferences that his wife was crazy. He'd been married to the woman for forty-some-odd years, he'd tell people, and God knows she had her crotchets. But as far as he was concerned if she said she saw a naked man, she saw a naked man, and it ate away at him when people took to treating him like a widower, when one woman even brought him a casserole.

Mrs. Jasper must have sensed her neighbors' growing skepticism as children darted along the street again and families recklessly barbecued on their river view patios. She began to call people, my mother among them, trying to keep the alarm from fading. She had *too* seen a naked man, she'd insist in a cracking voice. Anyone who doubted it did so at his own peril, she said, for there was no telling when he would return, and when he did — and he was going to — nobody would be safe. Of course, these calls only made things worse.

Late one September afternoon, Mrs. Jasper was in her kitchen, preparing a compress, when, out of the corner of her eye she saw something move outside her window. Afraid of being seen, she crept up and peered down at the river in time to see the naked man again, floating as before in a Disney mask, and waving. This time she did not shriek, nor dash for the phone, but watched the man carefully as he slipped downstream, pulling branches out of his way, twinkling in the sun.

Mrs. Jasper turned and tiptoed to the phone and dialed Mrs. Prosciutto, who lived next door downriver.

"The naked man has returned," Mrs. Jasper announced, "just as I had foretold."

Mrs. Prosciutto, who had lately taken to refusing calls from Mrs. Jasper, sighed wearily. "Now, don't get started," she said. "Get a hold of yourself, dear."

"I tell you, I have a hold of myself," Mrs. Jasper replied. "Look for yourself."

Mrs. Prosciutto considered pretending to look, just to humor the poor woman, but there was something in Mrs. Jasper's voice that compelled her to go to her window and look. There, indeed, drifted a naked man, slapping at a bug.

This being Mrs. Prosciutto's first glimpse of the naked man ("of *any* naked man except Angelo," she later claimed), she had Mrs. Jasper hang up, called the police, and, sobbing, locked all her doors and windows.

Again, by the time the police arrived, the man was nowhere to be seen. Though two women had now seen him, the police searched half-heartedly, tired of the whole business, and returned to headquarters within the hour.

That evening there was to be a development association picnic at the little beach that had been bulldozed out of the bank of the river. It was one of those events that lacked a core — no saints were honored, no harvest celebrated — and it always rang kind of hollow. The children arrived early, as the barbecue pits were being fired, and a game of kick-the-can developed. Children roamed along the water's edge looking for hiding places. The best hiding place was among the reeds, where it was shallow enough to wade, and it was there that Missy and Ricky Atherton chanced upon Mr. Jasper, crouched in his rowboat and pulling on his clothes.

Lift Your Feet

"Nature abhors a vacuum."
                    Ancient Physical Maxim

ALL HER LIFE, my mother wanted busy children. Nothing infuriated her more than the sight of one of her offspring lying around, staring into space. But she had a conflicting ambition which proved paramount: that her house remain at all times tidy and hygienic, that it exhibit, in effect, as little evidence of human activity as possible.

You could turn your back for a moment in my mother's house, leave a half-written letter on the dining room table, a magazine open on the chair, and turn around to find it had been "put back," as my mother phrased it, "where it belonged."

My wife, on one of her first visits to my mother's house, placed on an end table a napkined packet of cheese and crackers she had made for herself and went to the kitchen to fetch a drink. When she returned, she found the packet had been removed. Puzzled, she set down her drink and went back to the kitchen for more cheese and crackers, only to return to find that now her drink had disappeared. Up to then she had guessed that everyone in my family held onto their drinks, sometimes with both hands, so as not to make water rings on the end tables. Now she knows better.

These disappearances had a disorienting effect on our family. We were all inclined to forgetfulness, and it was common for one of us, upon returning from the bathroom and finding that every evidence of his work-in-progress had vanished, to forget what he'd been up to. "Do you remember what I was doing?" was a question frequently asked, but rarely answered, for whoever turned to address himself to it ran the risk of having his own pen, paper, book, tatting, suddenly disappear into the order of my mother's universe.

Every house has its own fragrance or stench, depending. My best friend's house always smelled of his mother's inevitable tuna casseroles and toll house cookies. My grandparents' home smelled of pine pillows, and cologne, and mildew, and ancestral foundation garments, and moth balls. But our house was distinctive in that its aroma varied dramatically from room to room. The living room smelled of "Brasso" and floor wax, the dining room of Lemon Pledge, the kitchen of Mr. Clean and bug spray, the bathrooms of Air-Wick and powdered cleansers. Indeed, the only room in which there remained some hint of human residence was my father's study, where Lysol could never quite obliterate the lingering overcast from his Burmese cheroots.

As my mother bustled through the house, spray cans ablast, I wondered if one day all her cleaning compounds would combine into a lethal gas, or spontaneously combust, leaving her dazed and wild-eyed, still vacuuming amid the rubble of her exploded household.

Filth had an animate form in my mother's mind. It was the beast lurking just beyond the hearth, ready to spring should the flames subside.

It did not help that we lived for a time in Chicago, where the soot used to sift into the house at such a rate that by evening, no matter how much cleaning my mother had done, you could write your name in the stuff on the window sills. When we moved to India, where we had servants to take care of the cleaning, my mother, instead of accepting this as a respite from her warfare with dirt, concentrated her efforts on germs. She began to see, in every bruised banana, in every nicked papaya, the death of her children.

And in fact I did almost die early in our stay from a delirious, skull-firing disease I picked up from a fly over lunch at school. I came out of my coma a convert to my mother's phobia, and it got so that when I turned on the faucets in the bathroom I could all but hear bacteria the size of bees whirring out of the pipes and up my nostrils in a great dry flow, and nesting in my lungs to sting and gnaw and whatever else it took to finish me off. The organisms I saw across my field of vision when I stared up at the sky, translucent, elongated beasties drifting along the dome of my eyeball, convinced me that I, alone among men, could see germs, and that hour by hour they were slipping under my eyelids and raging through my brain.

In those days it was customary for American households in New Delhi to bathe all their fruits and vegetables in something called "pinky water," a mixture of
water and potassium permanganate, which, later studies
were to show, had no effect on bacteria. It was a custom
their Indian employees took in stride. They had their
rituals, we had ours. In fact, considering their fondness
for colored water and powdered dyes, they probably
had a special understanding of pinky water. They were
nonetheless alarmed when, at dinner one evening, we
were commanded to spit out our green beans after it had
been discovered that they had not been sufficiently
pinkied.

My mother was not one of those raving memsahibs
who line up their servants three times daily to inspect
their fingernails. But she did have her doubts about her
staff's vigilance in matters immaculate. She once commanded our bearer, whose Hinduism prevented him
from taking life, to rid the house of flies, and returned
to find him dancing through the verandah, trying to
shoo them out the screen door with little flaps of his
dusting cloth. When she took on the exterminating role
herself, she was stopped one day by our Christian
driver, Peter John, whose Hindu heritage had not quite
worn out. "Madam," he asked her gently as she set off a
bug bomb in the storage room, "why do you kill flies?"
"Because," she explained, "they carry germs and germs
cause sickness." "Ah, but Madam," Peter replied conspiratorially, "you and I are Christians, and don't believe such things."

Nor could my mother depend on her children. How
were we to refuse the odd little silver-foiled milk sweets

we were offered in Indian households, or the freshly cut sugar cane which was sold along the road, or the chapati and curry Peter would offer us when we visited his quarters behind the house?

In our side yard in New Delhi there was a spigot which jutted up from the ground itself, and if I overcame a morbid preoccupation with disease it was because of the fine, silvery blade of water which continually leaked from its mouth, mucking the dust below. I knew that it was piped in unfiltered from the Jumna River, in which bones, ashes, whole cadavers freely floated from the ghats and slums and villages that lined its banks. But that didn't matter. And I knew that there was plenty of safe water to be had from the refrigerator, where sealed thermos pitchers of filtered, boiled ice water were kept. But that wasn't the same. I wanted to drink as the gardener drank, standing in the sunlight with water spattering my shirt front and wetting my chin as it fountained up from the ground.

Which is not to say that once I had drunk my fill I did not then furtively retire to the verandah to await my fate. I knew that I had made my tender insides available to all manner of larva, bacterium, virus, amoeba, fungus, worm, germ, and hobgoblin, and I'd sit and listen as the water gurgled through my belly for some tiny insect battle chatter, for the closing of pincers or the grinding of mandibles. I never heard them, suffered no ill effects I know of, and survived to regard my mother's terror of disease with unseemly skepticism.

My mother grew up in a brick house in western Pennsylvania, where her father was a Presbyterian minister.

He was a sweet man, but grave, and the household was always under the watchful gaze of the deacons of the church, whose lipless, disapproving faces oversaw my mother's nightmares for much of her life. The house was dark, the curtains half drawn, the woodwork heavy, the wallpaper somber and dense, the lamplight dim. My grandmother had a precarious disposition and a fearful, overextended concept of sin. Her housekeeping was minimal and sporadic; everywhere there was the clutter of a hundred interrupted chores: Sunday-school papers lying half corrected on the dining table, a broom leaning in the front hall, beds unmade, dishes unwashed in the kitchen sink. It was the sort of congested domestic chaos whose implicit message was that all human labor was futile against the engulfing tide of earthly sin and tribulation.

My mother worshipped her father, collided with her mother. My grandfather's boyhood had been spent in an immaculate household run by his mother, an illiterate German immigrant whose disposition was as sunny as her scrubbed and ordered kitchen. My mother sensed that her father was greatly pained by the disorder of his own household, and so on those days when it was due for a visit from the elders of the church, or from their smug, judgmental wives, and my grandmother had withdrawn to her room to rail alone against the injustices of her lot, my mother, even as a tiny child, would take it upon herself to tidy up.

So she would stack up all the back issues of church magazines, stuff all the sheet music into the piano bench, snatch up the little tumbleweeds of hair and dust which drifted across the floor, scoop up all the rubber bands, pencil stubs, paper clips, hymnals, notes, coats, boots, and brooms, and create, for the duration of the elders' visit, a precarious illusion of order and well-being.

Since melancholy was the prevailing mood in her disordered girlhood home, my mother began to equate order and cleanliness with peace and happiness. That the pursuit of order and cleanliness might impinge on her peace and happiness would not occur to her until late in life. In this instance, as far as she was concerned, the end justified the means. And in her few moments of leisure, sipping a cocktail and watching the news as her cooking timer ticked beside her, or chewing dietary toast and celery at lunch, she would sometimes gaze around at her shining, white-walled home, inhale the delicious scent of ammonia and polish, almost hear the harmonious disposition of her family's possessions throughout the house, and experience a rush of feeling which is reserved for those who are, no matter how hard they may fight it, deeply religious by nature.

I wouldn't have known what to do with all that background information even if I had had it. I always had the feeling her cleaning was somehow directed at me, and, often enough, it was.

Enraged to find me stretched out on the sofa, arms folded, eyes unfocused, mind blank, my mother would start in by asking, "Don't you have anything better to do?"

I always gave this question a lot of thought before finally replying, "What?"

"I said, 'Don't you have anything better to do?' "

"Anything better to do?"

"That's right."

Well, that was a silly question. Of course I had something better to do. Everybody had something better to do. *My mother* had something better to do. That wasn't the point. But before I could engage her in a discussion of the wide ranging implications of her inquiry, she would flee in exasperation. Sometimes she would go do errands, leaving the house deliciously quiet, leaving me to half an hour at least of utter inactivity, of watching the dust settle comfortably around me and listening to the refrigerator hum.

But more often she would begin to clean. From a distant corner of the house I would hear cupboards being opened, drawers being slammed shut. "Can't you stop leaving drawers open wherever you go?" was one of her most impassioned pleas. Her voice broke when she said it. Now that I think about it, it doesn't seem like such a big deal, but at the time it did. I'd get this tilting sensation in my stomach when she said it. Why *couldn't* I stop leaving drawers open wherever I went, I'd ask myself ashamedly, turning to face the lap of the sofa. What the hell was wrong with me that I couldn't stop leaving drawers open wherever I went?

Then there would be a silence, a doomed, tense stillness, until I began to make out the noise of her dusting. Her dusting was not the gentle caress of a soft cloth but the angry whipping of torn, discarded slips and undershorts across the imperceptibly dusty surfaces of the house. This slapping sound, and the occasional hiss of a cleaning spray, would approach until at last she was back in the living room, darting from furnishing to furnishing, growing ever more dishevelled as the house grew more immaculate around her. Finally she would near me with her smudged, flickering flag and crack it across the side tables, the lamps, the ash trays, until, unable to stand it any longer, I would make a major concession and sit up.

To my mother, of course, this was not a concession at all, but yet another sign of my insolence and decaying moral fibre. So she would withdraw for a while to prepare her heaviest artillery for the final assault.

I knew what was coming. As soon as I heard her vacuum cleaner start up I knew she was going to win. But I always tried to hang on, in the faint but persistent hope that this time I could outlast her.

Whether it was her headlighted, puff-bellied, droning old Hoover or her streamlined, sled-tracked, terrible-trunked Electrolux, I could tell where she was in the house by just listening. *Fmmmm,* she was on the carpet in the study. *Brrrr,* she had reached the bare hallway floor. *Thump, thump, thump,* she was making her way down the stairs. *Screech,* she was moving the dining room chairs from under the table.

By the time she reached the living room I would already be poised on the edge of my seat, jaw working, stomach revolving, shoulders high about my ears. By now she would be in a rage, running her machine across the floor with ferocious jerking motions, flupping up the corners of the carpet, sucking up all the detritus of my habitation, until finally she was within range, her eyes feverish with victory, and she let loose her ultimate war cry, the command that still puts an end to my recumbency, "Andrew, lift your feet!"

My mother's cleaning seems to have come to a head while I was in college. She started to get terrible head-

aches and psychosomatic digestive problems. Pretty
soon, she hired some cleaning women to come in every
week. They were Teutonic, like her grandmother, and
did a good job, and she was delighted to find that she
didn't have to clean up after them half so much as she
had cleaned up after her family. My sister has developed a second-hand passion for clean windows, and my
brother does the vacuuming in his house, perhaps to
avoid having to be the one to lift his feet. I try not to
think about it too much, but I have lately taken to cleaning the baseboards once a week. I figure if you don't
keep after them they'll just get filthy, and then where
will we be?

Class Dismissed

MY HOUSE IN RIVERSIDE was so far from Greenwich that I had to take a train to get to the high school. It was probably appropriate that a commuter's son should ride the rails to school, but it wasted a lot of time, especially if the trains were late, which they usually were. I was always getting to homeroom after the morning bell, breathless after the climb from the station.

My homeroom was overseen by Miss Godenhaus, a youthful language teacher who favored boys. "You are tardy again, my Andrew," she said as I darted toward my desk. "You are such a naughty, naughty boy." Homerooms were assigned alphabetically, and through some oversight Miss Godenhaus had been put in charge of students whose names she couldn't pronounce. Every morning we would begin the day hearing ourselves identified as "Valters," "Vard," "Ventvorth," and "Vhipple."

The main reason we gathered in homerooms was to hear the day's announcements. These were delivered over the P.A. system by Mr. Flyhope, the vice principal, who had a hot-off-the-wire style that lent urgency to even the most trivial directives.

"Something has just been handed to me from the woodshop," he'd tell us, rustling papers by the microphone. "Due to a mishap with one of the lathes, Bowl Turning Club will not meet this afternoon. Here's a note from Maintenance — anyone caught riding the rolling mop buckets down the halls will be severely disciplined. Locker Neatness Day is just a week off, G.H.S.ers, so let's hop to it. A word from Principal Bolger — he's been noticing a rise in dress code violations and wants the girls to know he's going to be keeping a sharp eye on hems. And boys, don't think you're fooling anyone by inking your sneakers."

My first class was English Literature and Composition. It was held in one of the third floor classrooms and taught by a large, rumpled man named Mr. Clemons. He had a hunted, Lon Chaney look, and ducked out of class every twenty minutes to "check on the commotion in the hall," or "borrow some chalk," only to return red-eyed and reeling. On his best days he was not a bad teacher, especially if you got him going on Jack London, whom he had seen as a boy. "Off he went," he told us, putting down *The Call of the Wild* and staring out the window, "leaving every comfort behind him for the freedom of the tundra."

But his good days were infrequent. Sometimes he was so incapacitated that he couldn't write the next day's assignment on the blackboard, and his scrawl would droop off onto the wall. When we all came in the next day, having failed to decipher his scribble and complete the assignment, he would rage at us and have us sit at our desks in silence for the rest of the period as he sat back, gazing at the ceiling and making windy noises through his teeth.

Part of the English requirement was a two-week speech course taught by a gigantic, bellowing woman named Miss Justin. To keep her voice projection demonstrations from disturbing other classes, she had been assigned a basement room between a boys' lavatory and a trophy case. She always talked at the top of her voice, and liked to kick off each class with a recitation of her own, which she would preface by saying, "Remember, this is all coming from my diaphragm." Her favorite writer was Tennyson, and she once got so whipped up reciting from *Idylls of the King* that she didn't notice that her undershorts had broken loose and fallen slowly to her ankles.

Our grade in speech was based on a recitation from memory of a work of our own choosing. I put off the assignment for a while; the recitations proceeded alphabetically, and I figured that it would be days before my turn came. However, a virus swept through school one morning, knocking several students in the T through V range off the roster, and suddenly Miss Justin was standing over me, asking what my selection was going to be.

In academic matters I was never able, as my mother put it, to "take a bird's eye view," so being unprepared for school was nothing new. Usually, I was pretty straightforward about it, but this time I was so awed by Miss Justin's proportions that I decided to fake it.

"I have chosen for my text," I blurted, heading for the lectern, "Sir Basil Pillsbury's *Ruminations on the Divine*." Of course, this was as much of a surprise to me as it was to Miss Justin; in fact, everything I did for the next few minutes surprised me.

"While oft in winter's bloom we saunter," I began, my eyes fixed on the clock, "amid the pale wreckage of autumnal splendor, when harvest moon shines on the tousled firmament to abridge the satyr's curséd wile . . ."

I went on like this, my voice rising and falling, until at last I hit on something that sounded final. There was a silence as I returned to my desk, and Miss Justin sat perfectly still, staring at me.

"Those," she said with uncharacteristic softness, "are words to live by."

English was followed by a class called Problems of Democracy. Politics were always being discussed around my house, so I enjoyed Problems of Democracy, and did fairly well. My teacher was a young Yale graduate named Mr. Renaldo who was considered an innovator. Chief among his innovations — and this was an earthquake at Greenwich High — was arranging all the desks in a circle, so he could pace around and draw everyone into the discussion. The only trouble with this was that it gave the boys an unhindered view of the girls as they crossed their legs, stretched, tucked in their blouses, brushed their hair, and a lot of us kept losing the drift of our arguments.

One boy who was not disturbed by these distractions was Alden Mack, an overachiever with geriatric political views. As far as I was concerned, Alden Mack was democracy's biggest problem and we were always baiting each other across the classroom. A patch of his hair had turned white, and he wore his National Honor Society pin on his sweater vests and carried a briefcase and always stood up for business, or, if the discussion were abstract, for money, of which he had quite a little. His argument against desegregation, for instance, was that it would cost too much. What would become of all those "colored only" facilities? Were they to be scrapped? "Gentlemen, I ask you," he intoned, "is that any way to run a railroad?"

I was never good at arguing with someone whose views were diametrically opposed to mine, and Alden Mack used to cut me to ribbons. Angry, frustrated, righteous, I was reduced to ambushing him after class, making fun of his briefcase, loudly speculating that his white patch had sprouted up out of the lobe of his brain which concerned itself with politics.

"Andy, Andy, Andy," he'd say, hurrying away, "let's try to behave like mature adults."

After Problems of Democracy I descended to a dim room on the first floor for Algebra II with Mr. Rider. I had no business taking Algebra II. I had no business taking Algebra I, for that matter, and passed it only because of a last-chance, extra-credit term paper on Charles Proteus Steinmetz. No one could explain to me what adding minuses meant, or why it was necessary, which left factoring, combining like terms, and all the rest of it, completely beyond my reach.

Mr. Rider's class was about as low as you could get in the college preparation program. The next stop, for those who flunked his course, was Distributive Education, or — worse — Industrial Arts, from which there was no return. Mr. Rider was an old, thin-lipped man with Truman glasses, and his primary teaching tool was shame. He took a special pleasure in calling on the least prepared among us to "come on up here and clean up this equation for us," or, "tick off those coefficients for the rest of the class." As we perspired before the blackboard, chalk poised uselessly, he would lean back and chuckle with satisfaction.

He also enjoyed reading our grades aloud (and the further he got from A+, the louder he read) but his most insidious technique was to have us correct each other's papers. All through the room, after one of his quizzes, friendships and romances crumbled as we X'ed each other's answers and calculated each other's sorry scores.

None of this taught us anything, except to avoid Mr. Rider and despise ourselves. "You're the worst class yet!" he once exulted, his eyes bright with accomplishment.

Biology was next, and it wasn't much better. The teacher, a monotonal man named Wilmer, started us off on the basic stuff, but, as in every science, the basic stuff was the most complicated and meaningless. I tried to keep up with all those pistils and stamens, enzymes and hormones, but I could never see how they all fit together into something recognizable, like a dandelion, or a duck.

Mr. Wilmer's idea of teaching was to point at a chart and call everything "Mister." "So Mr. Artery runs down from Mr. Aorta and into Mr. Hilum over here on the medial surface of Mr. Kidney." He hoped that by talking this way he would give the subject a vivid, True-Life Adventure quality, but it made everything sound like a phone book.

The bane of Mr. Wilmer's existence was a solemn boy named Richard Walters, who had been studying biology as a hobby since his fifth or sixth birthday. When Walters couldn't actually correct Mr. Wilmer, he liked to expand on his explanations.

"Excuse me, sir," he'd say, shooting his hand up and furrowing his brow, "but wouldn't you say that there's considerable doubt as to why the number of renal pyramids ranges from eight to twelve?"

Mr. Wilmer would look wistfully at his chart, turn around and sigh. "I don't believe so," he'd say. "At least, *I'm* not aware of any."

"That's funny. I believe there was a paper on the subject by Dr. Fritz Scheibwasser just a few years ago. I read about it in *Renal American*."

"Is that a fact?" Mr. Wilmer said with a clenched smile. "Perhaps you'd be kind enough to share Dr. Schweinwas — "

"*Scheib*wasser, sir. Dr. Fritz Scheibwasser."

"Scheibwasser, of course. Perhaps you'd share his findings with the rest of the class?"

"Well, I believe he traced it to genetic origins, if I'm not mistaken."

"Did he indeed? Well, I'm sure the rest of the class is fascinated to hear that. Now, if I might — "

"I'm surprised you missed it, sir. It made quite a splash in the Christmas issue."

"Well, you know, with the rush and everything . . ."

"If you like, I'll bring it in for you. I keep all my back issues."

"That would be really wonderful, Mr. Walters. Now, if I may be permitted to get back to what I was talking about. So then Mr. Interlobular Artery goes down here to . . ."

The rest of us encouraged Walters in his pedantry, because he never brought up anything we were supposed to know, and during his exchanges we could all relax and think of other things.

As the year progressed I got more and more behind in biology and gave up taking notes. This left me free to gaze upon the loveliness of Pamela Price, who, due to assigned seating, sat one desk up in the row beside me. She never said anything, but just sitting there, doing her nails or writing notes with her daisy-topped ball point, Pamela Price taught me more about biology than Mr. Wilmer ever could. Over the weeks I grew infatuated with her, and followed her through the halls, inhaling her latest fragrance, until the day we all got our report cards and she broke her silence.

"You know what that fuckah gave me in English?" I heard her whine to a beehived friend. "A *E!*"

The cafeteria at Greenwich High wasn't big enough to seat everyone, even when we ate in shifts, so we had to rush to lunch to avoid having to sit on the hallway floor. For a modest price, hot lunches were available, dished out by hair-netted women in marinara-spattered uniforms. But it wasn't easy reaching a table with your food intact. Oversized youths used to form a gauntlet near the cash register and snatch potato chips, french

fries, Eskimo Pies from passing trays. The only kid who
always got through safely was a strange, red-headed boy
who talked in monster voices and, as soon as he was
served, sprayed his food with spit.

I had Physical Education after lunch, which was hard
on the digestion. People were always throwing up during laps, prompting Coach Odarizzi to inquire sympa-
thetically, "Whatsamatter? You a sissy or something?"

Coach Odarizzi wore tastefully coordinated sweat
outfits and tended to go into furies. He was a great
believer in punishing the whole class for the transgres-
sions of one of its members, and many of our classes
were devoted to punitive exercises. One of these involved having us all stand with our arms out, crucifix
fashion, for extended periods. One of my classmates, an
asthmatic honor student named Westerberg, fainted
during one of these sessions and fell to the floor like a
phone pole, arms still outstretched. In extreme rages,
Coach Odarizzi would line us all up along a wall and
throw tennis balls at our backs. Since we were always
arranged according to height, the coach would either
start off with me (in which case his aim was poor but his
arm was strong) or finish with me (his aim perfected,
his arm depleted).

He was especially vigilant in the showers, where he
would stand with a clipboard, asking each of us as we
hunched by, "Did you soap your pits? Be sure you
soaped your pits."

Miss Godenhaus was my French teacher, and it was a
good thing, too, or I never would have passed. She let
up on boys, came down hard on girls, especially Alice

Dorman, who knew the language coming and going but had terrible pronunciation. "How grating to my ears," Miss Godenhaus would complain after one of Alice's grammatically perfect recitations. "Come my Andrew, and speak to me the way you do."

I knew next to no grammar, and not much more vocabulary, but my accent was impeccable, and all I had to do to please Miss Godenhaus was deliver long, nonsensical monologues.

"Venay assont mideau aron sur la terranmont fussé agronomy au leaux bassant cardé, pour la fountain d'un triseau," I'd tell her, and she would listen with her eyes shut, moving her head as if to music.

Some days I had Health and Hygiene seventh period. Health and Hygiene was dispensed by a short, moralizing man named Mr. Pezzafola. The classes were segregated according to gender, and wild rumors circulated among the boys as to what went on in the girls' classes. Those rumors were about all that kept the mind alive in Mr. Pezzafola's class. He turned out to be hopelessly confused about the difference between reproductive and digestive organs, which left a lot of us horrified, and he skipped over most of the best stuff by telling us, "You'll find out about that soon enough," or, "This is no place for that kind of talk."

He was fascinated by his own ailments, and once, as he described some kind of treatment he was taking for an inflamed colon, a slight boy named Skinner threw up on his desk.

"Mr. Pezzafola, Mr. Pezzafola," the boy beside him called out. "Skinner puked."

"Young man," replied Mr. Pezzafola, "I will not

have you using that sort of language in this classroom."

Other days I wound up the afternoon in Male Chorus. The music program at the high school had once been extraordinary, due to Mr. Theodore, an intimidating choral director who could wring music from a stone. But Mr. Theodore left before my senior year, leaving in his place a piping, florid man named Saucy. Dearborn Saucy.

Male Chorus could not have met at a worse time. It was open to everyone, and a lot of kids took it to avoid study hall. After six periods of confinement and abuse, a lot of these youths were ready for bear, or, at the very least, for Mr. Saucy.

"Boys, boys, boys," he'd implore with a twitchy grin as raspberries blasted through our renditions of "Goin' Home" and "MacNamara's Band." "Come *on* now. We're not going to get anywhere with *that* sort of behavior, *are* we?"

But things always went from bad to worse. Pens, protractors, Pez dispensers, cigarettes hopped around us like locusts. "Clutch" Szymanski began to make automotive noises in the tenor section, while Louis Parotti crawled among the basses, barking like a dog.

"*Pianissimo,* boys," Mr. Saucy cried, desperately conducting the meek and attentive in the front row.

But he couldn't ignore the uproar forever, and eventually he stopped waving his arms around, put his hands on his hips, stamped his foot and declared, "You boys had best watch yourselves, now, because in just two shakes I'm going to get stern."

"In just two shakes I'm going to get stern," Parotti mimicked, shaking his finger at "Clutch" Szymanski.

"Very well, then," Mr. Saucy said, his eyes blurring,

"if that's the way you want it," and he started to head for the door to get the principal.

"Aw, now," Parotti said expansively. "Come on. We don' mean no harm. We *like* you, Mr. Saucy. You're a good guy."

Mr. Saucy paused and looked back at Parotti with pained hope.

"Sure. I ain't kidding. Hey, Clutch. Wasn't I just saying what a great guy Mr. Saucy is?"

"Vroom. Vroom, eeeee. Vroom, vroom."

"See?"

Mr. Saucy turned back from the door. "Well . . ."

"Hey," Parotti said. "I tell you what. Why don't you hit that note for us? That way, we'll know there's no hard feelings."

His first day on the job, Mr. Saucy had made the mistake of demonstrating his remarkable ability to hit high C. Somehow he never realized that the feat had diminished him, and with touching eagerness he complied with every request to repeat it.

"Well, O.K.," he said. "If you really want to hear it."

"Are you kidding?" Parotti exclaimed, leading his friends in applause. "We want to hear Mr. Saucy hit his note, don't we?"

And so everyone would sit in appalled silence as Mr. Saucy's tremulous falsetto squeaked its way up the scale: "no-nee-*noo*-nee-nah, no-nee-*noo*-nee-nah, no-nee-*noo*-nee-nah," up into oblivion.

Offsides

MY HEIGHT MIGHT HAVE afforded a natural athlete some magnificent opportunities, but my growth rate always seemed to me ominous, like the overextension of a rubber band. In the mirror at night I would examine with growing alarm the stretch marks which cross-hatched my middle like tribal tattoos, and I had a nightmare once in which I actually split apart and had to be patched together with special elastic substances. My bedroom was a half refurbished cellar rec area in a home of niggardly construction. The acoustical-tiled ceiling was six feet high, and I was always parting my hair on the halo-shaped fluorescent light fixtures in the dark.

I was nearing my present height of six feet four inches by the tenth grade, and had been plagued throughout my boyhood by middle-aged men who mistook me for basketball material. I managed to avoid actual team sign-up sheets all through junior high school, but during my first senior high school gym class Coach Odarizzi took me aside and said, "Ward, with that height you could go places. Why don't you take your glasses off and live a little?"

Somehow I found the coach's call to action irresistible. While I was not about to dispose of my glasses (which were crucial to any slim hope of success I might have had) I did in fact show up for the first junior varsity practice that year.

After the usual setting-up exercises, we were instructed as to our first passing pattern. Three of us were to stand side by side at the starting line, the man in the middle holding the ball. When the whistle blew, each man was to weave in among the others, throwing the ball to the man passing directly in front. I am still a little shaky on how it was supposed to work. I guess it was like braiding, or maybe square dancing. In any case, I was in one of the first trios, and when the whistle blew, and I was passed the ball, I kind of zigzagged across the court in no particular pattern, throwing the ball at whoever was handy. I think at one point I threw the ball into the air and caught it myself, but I may be imagining that. In any case, after I had crossed the court in this fashion I continued to jog into the locker room, got dressed, went home, and never showed up for practice again.

I never could chin myself. Still can't, without taking a little leap to start with, which is cheating. Chinning was part of our high school physical fitness test, and when my turn came (we were to chin ourselves as many times as we could in thirty seconds) I would jump up, grab hold of the bar, and just hang there, for all intents and purposes, until my time ran out, or my hands slipped, or Coach Odarizzi told me to give it up.

"Work on that, Ward," he'd mutter, jotting something down on his clipboard. Perhaps "jotting" is not the word for it; the coach was a laborious penman and tended to bite down on his tongue as he wrote.

I suppose Richard Walters, who was almost a hundred pounds overweight, had a harder time of it than I did. He would spend his thirty seconds jumping up and down beneath the bar in a vain effort to reach it, as the coach solemnly stood by with his stop watch.

We usually kicked off gym class by climbing ropes to the gymnasium ceiling. I was started off on the smooth, knotless ropes, but after a few floor-bound, rope-burned days I was shown to the one knotted rope, before which I cued up with the anemic, the obese, and the cowardly, who could not have made it up a ladder, let alone a rope.

I would grab hold of the rope and then, as I dangled, try to get it tangled with my legs. Within seconds, I would get this draining feeling in my arms and down I would slide to the floor, folding up like a spider. The coach sometimes said I wasn't trying, but he never noticed how the pits of my elbows hollowed during rope climbing, sure evidence of my exertion.

I don't think I was ever the very last to be chosen for gym class teams, but I was usually among the last three or four. This group included Richard Walters, who had about as much trouble getting around as chinning, a nearly blind boy named Merritt Hull who was always losing school days to a urinary-tract disorder, and an eruptive menace named Norenski, who frequently fell into rages, kicking at groins when anyone tried to tell him what to do. By the time the choice was narrowed down to this foursome, one of the captains would say, "What the hell, at least he's tall," and I'd be chosen.

I still don't know what "offsides" means, and I avoid all games in which the term is used. I played soccer once in summer camp, but only because I had to, and every few days someone would shout that I was offsides. I would always apologize profusely, and stomp around kicking at the turf, but I never knew what they were talking about.

Football huddles were a source of mystery and confusion for me. There would always be a short, feisty character who called the plays. I rarely had much of a role in these plays, and usually wound up somewhere on the line, half-heartedly shoving somebody around.

But I do remember a time when, in a desperation move, the captain selected me to go out for a long one. I guess the reasoning was that no one on the opposing team would have ever suspected me of such a thing. I was told, in the odoriferous hush of the huddle, that I was to break formation on 24, try a lateral cutback on 47, head forward on hike, and then plunket closed quarters in a weaving "T" down the straightaway. That may not have been the precise terminology, but it might as well have been.

I think I ran in place on 24, turned 360 degrees on 47, was totally ignored on hike, ran a little way, and then turned in time to see both teams, it seemed, piling on top of the quarterback, who was shrieking, "Where are you? Where are you?" I suppose if I had gotten hold of the ball we might have managed a first down, but I don't know what that means, either.

The first gym teacher I remember was a soft-spoken and great-jawed man named Mr. Bobbins. Mr. Bobbins took me under his wing when I showed up in the middle of the seventh grade, the new kid from India. It was basketball season when I arrived, and the class was already pounding up and down the court, shooting hoops. "The idea here, Andy," Mr. Bobbins said when I confessed my ignorance of the game, "is to put the ball through the basket."

I had known that much, but found Mr. Bobbins so reassuring that I asked, "From the top or from underneath?"

"Definitely from the top," Mr. Bobbins replied gravely. "You won't get anywhere the other way."

My gym suits fit me only in sports shop fitting rooms. By the time I got them to school they'd be several sizes too small. I don't think I ever passed a happy hour in a gym suit, and at no time was I unhappier than during the week we had coed gymnastics. All the equipment was set up in the girls' gym, and I guess the Phys. Ed. department figured it would be logistically too difficult to have the boys and girls trade gyms for a couple of weeks. I prefer to believe that this arrangement was unavoidable, that no one thought it was a good idea. Nowhere was I flatter of foot, spindlier and paler of leg, more equivocal of shoulder, and heavier of acned brow than in the girls' gymnasium.

We would have to line up boy-girl-boy-girl in front of the parallel bars, and it was no picnic when my turn came. I could never straighten my arms on the parallel bars, and spent a lot of time swinging from my armpits and making exertive noises. Another exercise involved jumping over horses. We were supposed to run up to the things, grab them by their handles, and swing our legs over. This, it seemed to me, was an unreasonable expectation, and I always balked on my approach. "You're always balking on your approach," the girls' gym teacher would shout at me. "Don't balk on your approach." Thus lacking momentum, I would manage only to grab the bars and kind of climb over the things with my knees. My only comfort was in watching Richard Walters try to clear the horse, which he never did, even by climbing.

The balance beam was probably the least threatening piece of equipment as far as I was concerned. I had a fair sense of balance and enormous, clutching feet, and I could usually make it across all right. But when the exercise called for straddling, and my flaring shorts endangered coed decorum, I would pretend to slip from the balance beam and then hurry to the next piece of equipment.

Coed gymnastics was in some ways a mixed bag, for while there was always the agony of failing miserably and almost nakedly before the fair sex (as it was known at the time), we were afforded chances to observe the girls exercising in their turbulent Danskins. I hope I'll never forget how Janet Gibbs moved along the balance beam, how Denise Dyktor bounced upon the trampoline, how Carol Dower arched and somersaulted across the tumbling mats. Perhaps one of the true high points of my adolescence was spotting for Suzie Hawley, who had the most beautiful, academically disruptive calves in Greenwich High School, and who happened once to slip from the high bar into my startled and grateful clutches.

But that was a fleeting delight in a context of misery. Mostly I remember just standing around, or ducking from the end of one line to the end of another, evading the mortifications of coed gymnastics as best I could.

Wrestling class was held in the cellar of the high school on gray, dusty plastic mats. Perhaps it was the cellar that made these classes seem clandestine, like cock fights. We were all paired up according to weight. I think at one point I was six feet two inches and weighed 130 pounds, and I was usually paired up with five-foot two-inch 130-pounders, rippling little dynamos who fought with savage intensity. I would often start off a match by collapsing into a last-ditch defensive posture, spread-eagled on my belly, clutching at the mat. That way, no matter how much Napoleonic might was brought to bear on flipping me over for a pin, one of my out-stretched limbs would prevent it. I remember when one of my opponents actually burst into tears, because every time he managed to fold one of my limbs into an oper-able bundle, out would flop another, too distant to reach without letting go of the first. I may never have won a match this way, but at least I lost on points, not pins.

For eleven years, Physical Education had been an agony, but in my senior year I finally realized that I couldn't do any worse in it by not trying than I had done by trying. I took it upon myself to lighten things up when it seemed to me that everyone was getting worked up over nothing. I'd wink at opposing linesmen, do Gillette commercials between plays, stuff the ball under my shirt and accuse my teammates of getting me into trouble.

None of this went over well with the athletes among us, nor with Coach Odarizzi. "Knock it off, Ward," he'd call from the sidelines. "And grow up."

Playing games still comes up from time to time, and when it does, some of the old miseries return. I pass a couple of friends who are shooting baskets on an outdoor court. "Hey, Ward," one of them shouts. "Come on, Stretch. Let's see what you can do." I have mastered the weary shrug, the scornful wave, the hurried departure. But the ball is tossed my way — deftly, by a man who comes to my shoulders — before I can escape.

I make a pawing motion to gather it toward me, try to trap it in the hollow of my stomach. It rolls down my clamped legs, bounces upon one of my size fourteens, rolls listlessly away. I reach for it with a clapping movement, capture it between my palms, straighten up and sigh.

"O.K., Ace," someone shouts, "swish it in there."

"It's been a while," I say, giving the ball a tentative bounce. I squint over the top of the ball, regard the distant basket, hold my breath, and at last, with a hunching lunge, throw the goddamn thing.

It takes a direct route to the rim of the hoop, which makes a chattering noise on contact and sends the ball back in a high arc over my head. "Man," I say, lurching after it, "am I out of practice."

The Last Mambo

I HATED SCHOOL DANCES, and somehow I always wound up going to them with someone I didn't know very well. There was no way of getting to know girls at dances. The music was too loud, for one thing, and conversation had a way of doubling back on me.

"Clever how they've hung the crepe paper," I'd hear myself remark.

"I — I'm sorry?"

"I was just saying, 'CLEVER HOW THEY'VE HUNG THE CREPE PAPER!'"

This wasn't helped any by my habit of planting my dates directly in front of the bandstand. "This way," I'd say, staring up at Sal Fasalbo and His Pennies From Heaven, "we can get the full effect." Then, when the music demanded a dance step I couldn't handle, I'd pretend to be overwhelmed by the sound and just stand there, snapping my fingers.

Dancing never seemed to me to have anything to do with anything. Nobody got out on the floor to interpret spring, or make rain, or keep in shape. Body contact was about the only motivation I could think of, but none of the really flashy steps called for any. There were those who claimed they danced to get in touch with the music, but who wanted to get in touch with Sal and His Pennies, or Biff Tempter and the Tantrums, or any of the other bands that played our school?

All our dances had themes — Harvest Moon, Big Top, Roaring Twenties — which had to be carried through to the last decoration. Nobody thought it would be a good idea just to dim the gymnasium lights and dance. I was class artist in the ninth grade, and I was always getting talked into working on decoration committees. I wouldn't have minded this, but the committees were poorly funded and headed by a perky girl with Olympian expectations.

"I don't know how you guys feel about it," she'd tell us, "but I want this to be the best dance they've ever had at Eastern. I've got it all pictured in my mind. It's gonna be Winter Wonderland this time, right? So what we'll do is build a whole town. Kind of an Alpine town. Then we build this chimney around one of the ropes and Craig can dress up as Santa and come sliding down. And I know where we can get a real sleigh, too, and maybe even some reindeer, and I have a cousin who'd love to lend us some trees, and we can rent some stars and hang them from the ceiling and they'll just twinkle in the light and it'll be so exciting."

But sooner or later she would come down with something and disappear, and with her would vanish every hope of reindeer and starlight. So we'd have to make do with construction paper and thirty feet of streamers, two rolls of aluminum foil and a box of crayons.

Working on decoration committees did have its pluses, however. I was less terrified of girls when I worked with them on something. Conversation progressed naturally, and I could crack jokes without choking up. Among the girls I worked with — I was often the only boy on the decoration committee — was the Class Beauty, a high-spirited girl named Beth Wysock. "Wysock" seems an awkward handle at this remove, but at Eastern Junior High School it was a melodious sound, uttered with awe and longing.

Beth was hard working. She stayed with me through long afternoons of foil-slicing and paper-pasting, and she seemed to enjoy my company. So much so, in fact, that I began to entertain a crazy notion: that Beth Wysock might agree to go with me to the Ninth Grade Prom.

The idea snowballed into a kind of test I had to take if my life was going to mean anything. I wrestled with it for two days and nights, asked her out a hundred times before my mirror, tried out every conceivable phrasing, anticipated every possible response, until I could hold it off no longer.

What seemed to attract her to me was my sense of humor, so one afternoon I pulled out all the stops. I did Jonathan Winters routines. I impersonated Cagney. I did Chaplinesque things with the paper cutter. I put Ping-Pong balls in my socks and limped around the room. I had her laughing so hard she was doubled over, begging me to stop, and it was then, when she was my slave, that I asked her.

"So," I said, sobering suddenly and bowing, "how about if you and I went to the prom together?"

Perhaps it was the deadpan delivery, perhaps it was the little bow, perhaps it was the way my face twitched when I spoke, but this last gag was without doubt the funniest thing Beth Wysock had ever heard. She actually fell out of her chair laughing, and sat for several minutes, tears streaming down her perfect cheeks.

I wound up, again, going to the dance with someone I didn't know well. Beth Wysock went with Peter Watteau, the best dancer at Eastern Junior High School. Peter Watteau was, in fact, so socially precocious that some suspected he was a midget who had sneaked back to school in pursuit of a second chance. He wore ties and jackets and seemed to be free of shame, uncertainty, and blemish. Tucking his chin against his throat to lower his voice, he was capable of saying anything, from "Good day, gentlemen," to the boys, to, "You're looking very lovely today, Janet," to the girls, or in this case to the Janets.

It was customary, during each dance, to clear a space so everyone could stand around and watch Peter Watteau and his dancing partner demonstrate the Samba, the Bop, the Gavotte, whatever happened to be making the rounds. I didn't like Watteau, but I would stand around with the others and watch him mambo if it meant not having to dance, not having to talk, not having to do anything.

I tried to kill time at dances by fetching punch. My date for the Ninth Grade Prom, a prim, dumbfounded girl who was my alternate homeroom representative, downed seven cuploads before the evening was old. "Isn't it delicious?" I exclaimed as she drained her Dixie cups. "Here, I'll get you some more." Before she was finished swallowing I'd be back among the dancers again, excusing myself along a weaving route to the punch bowl.

Late in the evening the band struck up a Mambo, and a circle formed around Watteau and the unreachable Beth Wysock. Watteau lived for these moments. He had a move for every beat of the conga drum, every hiss of the maracas. Beth played a secondary role, dancing in place as Watteau did his business around her.

Everything went smoothly until a rowdy, held-back youth named Norenski decided he had had it up to here with Peter Watteau, broke into the circle, and began to cha-cha menacingly around him. Norenski's Brylcreemed friends, who lived in stucco houses along the river and stuck together like brothers, began to hoot from the sidelines.

"Hey, now," one of Watteau's colleagues called out, "let's not spoil everybody's fun." But this only seemed to fan the flames. All through the gym, Industrial Arts majors began making lewd suggestions.

Center stage, Beth Wysock had sensibly melted into the crowd, leaving Watteau mamboing in the spotlight. Norenski began to veer in close, pursing his lips and making kissing noises and having a wonderful time.

"Whoa, there, friend," we could hear Watteau say in a faulty baritone. "Let's take it a little easy, there."

But Norenski didn't seem to hear him, and finally came up behind Watteau and lifted him off the floor. Watteau offered no resistance and grinned rigidly, as if he were part of the prank. The band raggedly stopped playing, but Watteau kept his feet moving, and in the few silent moments he was carried around like that, still mamboing into the air like a dancing doll, Peter Watteau was ruined.

"Hey, everybody," he cried as Norenski walked away in triumph. "Let's really do some dancing!" But his hands shook and his voice broke and everyone turned away.

The rest of the evening was a letdown. Refusing punch and marching away from the bandstand, my date demanded that we dance two numbers. My parents were late picking us up and I had to stand in the parking lot with my quenched date for almost an hour, declining rides from chaperons.

Still, the Ninth Grade Prom is the only dance I remember with any pleasure. Beth Wysock went on to girls' school, but Peter Watteau didn't go on to much of anything. By the twelfth grade he was reduced to crashing sophomore Coca-Cola parties and making passes at girls two years his junior. "Say, Helen," he once said to my sister at one of these affairs. "I admire your spunk."

Hoods

RIVERSIDE, Connecticut, may not have been known for its tough kids, but it had its share. Only a few days after I got started at Eastern Junior High School, a substitute teacher named Fetters caught the sullen, volcanic Burns brothers smoking in the boys' room. Never ones to hang their heads in shame, they refused to accompany Mr. Fetters to the principal's office, preferring instead to stuff the small, shrieking man into a tall lavatory trash bin and roll him down the hall.

For some reason there hadn't been any tough kids in school with me in India. The only fight I had ever been in by the time I moved to Riverside was with a sour, lonely boy named Baron who was sensitive about his girth. He threw his punches with his eyes closed so that all I had to do was duck until he finally got tired of swinging, announced he had won, and marched away.

It took me weeks before I could begin to recognize which kids were tough at Eastern Junior High. After the Fetters affair I became desperately eager to learn how to avoid tough kids. "Now, how about that one?" I'd ask a classmate, pointing to a boy in the hallway. "Is he tough?" And invariably I'd be told, "Naa, that's Trevor Gilwick" — or Dickie Delage, or Tim Replogle. "He's a dipshit."

I learned whom to avoid by trial and error. One day, during gym class, I refused to give up a basketball to Nick Norenski. "Give me," he commanded as I dribbled by him.

"I don't think it's your turn," I replied brightly. "I'll let you have it when it's your turn."

"Give me now," he growled, suddenly hunching over as if to charge, "or I hit you."

Surely *this* was a tough kid, I thought, throwing the ball a little way into the air and then passing it to Norenski. "There, you see?" I said, backing off. *"Now* it's your turn."

Since a lot of reputations were built on punches thrown as far back as kindergarten, you really had to have grown up in Riverside to know which kids were dangerous. There were a lot of boys who had been tough as nails in second grade, but who had failed to match their classmates' growth rates and were stuck with reputations they could no longer defend. One of these was a flyweight named Tapping, who was always challenging the tallest kids in the college prep program to say something disparaging about his height. "I hear

you say something?" he'd bark with a furious, foamy
look in his eyes, grabbing a kid by the belt and pulling
himself up to his toes. "You got something to say to
me?"

Then there were the overaged, held-back kids like
Turk Tartaddio. I don't know if Turk Tartaddio ever
really did anything, but he had quite a reputation. Every
story that circulated about him was second or third hand,
and nobody dared try to verify anything with Turk himself. Turk had spent three years butting up against the
ninth grade, and he towered over the rest of us. It was
whispered that his recreation consisted of jumping up
and down on kids from Stamford. It was also said that
he was so proud of his girlfriend, a stocky, bubble-
topped girl who chewed her lacquered nails to the nub,
that he would sell Polaroids of her in various stages of
undress. Of course, none of us were willing to test this
rumor, since there was a fair chance that it was false,
and the other was true.

Turk could not have been very bright, since he hadn't
been held back for bad behavior so much as for just
sitting there, hunched over his little desk, laboriously
inking in the spaces in every a, b, d, e, g, o, p, q, and
capital R he could find in his frayed textbooks. The
teachers had pretty much given up on Turk, and when
his turn came in class they made drastic adjustments.

"And now, Mr. Tartaddio," our ninth-grade English
teacher once said during the first round of a spelling bee,
"if you would spell, uh, 'gun' for the rest of the class."

"You mean 'gun'?" Turk said. "Like you shoot
with?"

"Yes. 'Gun.' That's right."

"You want me to spell it?"

"If you would, yes."

"Gun. Jesus, I don't know," Turk said, reaching back and twisting his ducktail. "Hey, is there a 'g' in there?"

"Quite right, Mr. Tartaddio," the teacher said. " 'G' is the first letter. Then what? G . . ."

"Uh . . ."

". . . u . . ."

"Uh . . ."

". . . n. G-u-n. Gun. G-u-n. Thank you, Mr. Tartaddio. Now, Mr. Varner, if you would spell 'paraphernalia' for the rest of the class?"

Sammy Buono always followed close behind Turk Tartaddio. Buono looked a little like Paul Anka and was very big with girls who wore eye makeup. He was always picking fights with kids, but whenever someone accepted one of his challenges he would back off and threaten the kid with cousins. He claimed to have an army of them, and told anyone who threatened to so much as lay a hand on him that all he had to do was pick up the phone and within minutes Buono Golden Glovers from as far away as Far Rockaway would roar in, armed to the teeth and ready for anything.

Turk always ignored Buono's incitements and never backed him up when he got into trouble. One day Buono casually punched Roger Gains, a severely nearsighted and studious boy, in the deltoid. It was the sort of second-nature thing tough kids were always doing to passersby, but Gains proved deceptively strong and short-tempered, and seconds after Buono threw his knuckle punch he found himself flat on the floor with an altered nose.

"I knew it," Buono sputtered, rising to his knees and then falling backward. "I knew it would take two of you!"

The Untouchables was a big television hit when I was in high school. It was about Elliot Ness, a treasury agent in the Twenties who tried to bust up the Chicago mob. But the hero to a lot of the kids at Greenwich High was not Ness but Frank Nitti, who took over the syndicate when Capone went to jail. Nitti's greatest fan was Georgio Barome, a scrawny, ambitious kid who was always trying to organize a gang out of the bilious boys who lived along the river. Barome fancied himself as Nitti's reincarnation, and used to barge through the halls with a self-important air, humming *The Untouchables'* theme and snapping his fingers.

Barome never quite managed to form a gang. His boys kept falling out among themselves when it got down to designing a jacket and selecting a name. Still, they liked to hang around together, and showed up unannounced at social functions to jut their chins and throw their weight around.

Every now and then a kid would break a window in downtown Greenwich and editorials would appear in *The Greenwich Time* about getting the kids off the streets. A women's group would then set up a canteen in a church basement or a school gymnasium and funds would be collected for a discount phonograph, a couple of records, a Coke machine, a second-hand Ping-Pong table, and some boxes of checkers.

I went to a canteen one night when I was in the tenth grade. I decided to go because I had taken to lifting weights, and though viewed from the side I still could have been mistaken for a cutout, I had developed shoulders. They were nothing to write home about, but they beat what I'd had before, which were really just sloping extensions of my neck, and I wanted to see if they might get me somewhere in social situations. I hadn't been having much luck with girls, and hoped the canteen would be a low-key place where I could sit around, drawing them to me with quips.

The canteen was set up in an elementary school gym. It was full of kids, but none of them were doing anything, and probably would have had a better time in the streets. All but one of the checker sets were incomplete, so only one game was in progress, and a lot of kids just stood around watching. The records which had been donated to the canteen were outdated, and I remember that Doris Day's rendition of "Hawaiian Wedding Song" was playing when I came in. Nobody knew any steps to fit it, and it was hard to catch the rhythm because the phonograph needle kept skipping grooves. The only place to sit was on some bleachers which had been set up against one wall, and since everyone sat facing the same way it wasn't easy to socialize.

I spent the evening in a seat high above the gym, watching Barome and his boys break in on dancers. They didn't really want to dance so much as keep things fluid, and when Alberto Barome, Georgio's brother, kicked in a leg of the Ping-Pong table, the chaperon, a tall, smiling man named Walks, decided to quiet things down by abdicating his duties to Barome. Up to that point he had supervised the canteen by standing against a wall with his hands in his pockets and saying, "Boys, boys, boys," when things began to get out of hand. But now he said, "Georgio, I think it would be very constructive if you and your boys would see to it that the kids behave themselves."

"Hey, no problem," Barome said, twitching his shoulders. "Me and the boys'll see everyone acts nice."

Barome proved a stern taskmaster. As the evening wore on he and his friends developed a policy of making everyone sit in the bleachers who was not actually dancing or playing checkers, and it got to the point where you had to raise your hand if you wanted to go to the bathroom or get a Coke, or leave. Finally, late in the evening, a bored kid named Brewster stood up, exclaimed, "Who needs this?" and hurled a Coke bottle through a window. Mr. Walks called the police, everyone was told to go home, and the canteen was closed for good.

The strongest kid in Greenwich High School was a massive black named Stones Jones. He stood six feet six, and though in his early days he had blood-flowered a lot of noses and purpled a lot of eyes, by the end of his six years in high school he had enough respect for his own strength and disposition to keep pretty much to himself.

But every few months, like fledgling gunfighters, kids would try to test Stones's power, snarling their challenges up to him in piping voices.

"Aw, now," Stones once asked a slight, twitchy youth named Gumdeck, gently palming the top of his head and lifting him to the tips of his toes, "why can't we just be friends?"

"Hey, all right," Gumdeck squeaked back. "That'd be great."

Stones's supremacy especially galled Georgio Barome

and his followers. They never did anything more than some light shoplifting, but they were as close to hoods as we had at Greenwich High, and they knew that as long as Stones was in the picture they looked ridiculous.

So one night they got all worked up, guzzling beer and punching each other in the arm, and they finally crowded into a car and drove to The Touchdown Bar and Grill in Port Chester, where Stones liked to spend his evenings, sipping beer in solitude.

"All right, Stones," Georgio said, speaking for the group as they filed into the bar. "This is it."

Stones gave his beer a wistful look. "This is what?" he asked softly.

Barome looked back at his troops with some hesitancy. Even slumped on a bar stool, Stones towered over him, and in his hands his beer mug looked like a salt shaker.

"We're gonna teach you a lesson," Barome said, jutting his jaw.

Stones slowly turned around on his bar stool, and as he did, Barome and his five allies backed up a little. "What lesson is that, Georgie?" he wanted to know.

By then Barome must have realized that he had embarked on the most foolish project of his life, but he swallowed hard and said, "We gonna teach you who's on top, here."

Stones stared at him for a moment and shrugged. "All right," he said, turning back to his beer.

Barome watched as Stones sipped and, rocking on the balls of his feet, said, "All right, what?"

"All right, I'll take you on," Stones said, getting a little irritated now and crushing a peanut between his fingers. "But first I'm finishing my beer."

"All right," Barome said, backing out the door, "if that's the way you want it. We'll see you outside."

As the challengers waited in the parking lot for Stones to come out, Barome's younger brother, Alberto, made a move to kick Stones's gigantic Harley-Davidson.

"You crazy?" the others said, shoving Alberto aside, for they knew that Stones's relationship with his bike, the largest motorcycle in Fairfield County, was tender and intimate.

After reflecting for a moment on the sweetness of life, one of them took Georgio aside and said, "Hey, we showed him we wasn't taking any shit from him. Let's get the hell out of here."

But just then Stones appeared in the doorway, tucking his shirt beneath his two-lane belt, and belching. Barome gestured to his friends, and they fanned out, crouched, fists clenched, and for a moment the challenge looked almost plausible; there were six of them, after all, and only one Stones Jones.

"Hold on a minute," Stones said, walking over to his motorcycle. "Let me just get my hog out of the way."

"You better not be thinking about running off on that thing," Barome suggested hopefully.

"Aw, hell no," Stones said, reaching for his Harley. "I just don't want my hog to get scratched."

And with that he put one hand on the handle bars and one hand under the seat and without bending his arms, slowly lifted his motorcycle over his head. And by the time he had set it down a few feet out of harm's way, Georgio Barome and his boys were on their way home.

Maybe Georgio Barome, Turk Tartaddio, Stones Jones, and the rest wound up in jail, just as their teachers prophesied, but you never know. The last time I saw Barome he was working in a Sinclair station on the Boston Post Road. When I drove up to the pump he could not have been more polite, and in the background I could hear his friends' voices swooping falsetto through Four Seasons harmonies as they sat together in the garage, staring up into the fluorescent light.

And it wasn't Georgio, Turk, or Stones, but studious, responsible Dickie Delage, Dramatics Association Vice President and Oceanography Club cadet, who just the other day confessed at long last to having fired four bullets into the brain of a strolling school teacher beside the Taconic Parkway when he was just a dipshit and Barome was at his peak.

No Parking

MOST OF MY FRIENDS were in line for their driving licenses the day they turned sixteen, but I waited a while. I don't think it was driving that threw me. It was just that I was afraid of girls, and didn't want to do away with the last obstacle to dating them.

I tried having my parents drive me to dates, but it never worked out. I had a friend named Louis whose father used to sit in the front seat listening to phone-in radio shows while his son made out with his date in the back seat. But my parents were different. Nothing could pour water on an evening like having my parents drive me to and fro. My mother had a great many views on how her son should behave around young ladies, and gave me last minute tips as we drove up to my date's door.

"Now, remember to knock twice. Don't knock any rhythms. And don't say, 'Hi.' Say, 'How do you do, Mrs. So-and-so?' or 'Good evening, Mrs. So-and-so.' And remember to say something nice about Cindy's dress. And for gosh sake, stand up straight. Girls like nice, tall boys."

"I can't *do* anything with my parents driving," I used to tell my friends when they asked me why I wasn't dating. But as soon as I turned sixteen that excuse didn't hold any water and late in my junior year I finally signed up for driving lessons. I could have taken lessons at the high school, but I had this image of myself losing control in the parking lot and careening down onto the playing field, splintering bleachers as grades ten through twelve watched from the building above. So I signed up for classes at a Stamford concern called Cookie's Academy of Auto Safety.

Cookie, a hip-heavy man with spiky hair, emphasized politeness. "Courtesy is contagious" was his credo, and he tried to apply it to every driving situation. "Say you got a truck tailgating you at sixty, seventy miles an hour. What should you do? Well, first ask yourself, 'What's polite, here? What's the courteous way to handle this son of a bitch?' Just think along those lines and you can't go wrong."

Classes were held in a dank room over a transmission shop in downtown Stamford. Cookie liked to keep his classes freewheeling. "O.K.," he'd say, "anyone got any problems they want to talk about before we get started?"

Among my classmates was a fortyish woman named Mrs. Poldy who had taken the course five times before.

Mrs. Poldy always had problems she wanted to talk about, few of which had anything to do with driving, so we never would get started.

"I know it's crazy, talking about this with total strangers," she'd say, her eyes brimming, "but the kids have been absolute hell all week, and I just have to open up to somebody."

"Of course you do," Cookie told her, cradling her head. "People need people."

After a couple of sessions in parking lots, Cookie had me drive in the streets. "O.K., Andy," he said, gripping the door handle with both hands, "let's just ease her out into traffic." I did fairly well, except that I had trouble with my lefts and rights.

Cookie's car was equipped with a second brake pedal that he would pump whenever we neared trees. A tree had once fallen on a car Cookie was driving, and he had been terrified of trees ever since. "I don't see why they don't cut the bastards down," he used to tell me, his eyes large.

Cookie had a lot of girlfriends scattered around Stamford, many of them former students, and as I became more advanced he had me drive him to his assignations and left me in driveways to practice parking.

"I'm just going to settle up on something," he'd tell me, hurrying out of the car. "I'll be right in and right out."

Perhaps I never got the hang of parallel parking because I had practiced it alone in strange driveways. It was the only part of the driving exam that I worried about, but fortunately there were no parking spaces around the Department of Motor Vehicles the day I took the test, and the examiner decided to skip it. "I'm going to take a chance on you this time, Andy," he told me, signing something on his clipboard, "so don't ever disappoint me."

Now that I was licensed, nothing stood in the way of my taking girls out on dates. My best friend in high school was a well-organized, phlegmatic youth named Ed who had a clear idea of what he wanted from girls. At one time Ed actually asterisked his steady date's menstrual cycle on his appointments calendar so that he could beg off dates with her during inappropriate periods. I thought this was very sophisticated and admired Ed for his singlemindedness, though I didn't really know what menstrual cycles had to do with anything, and, in any case, was under the impression that all girls went through them on the twenty-eighth day of each month.

One of Ed's dates was an adoring and bountiful girl named Fredericka, whom he eventually gave up bothering to take to movies, parties, dances, or restaurants, preferring instead to proceed directly to Binney Park, where for hours on end they would battle over questions of access. Eventually, Ed tired of Fredericka, and, in a way, handed her over to me. I didn't have any idea what I wanted out of Fredericka, but suddenly there she was, and I asked her out.

I worked the evening out ahead of time down to the last detail. Keeping the ball rolling was my greatest challenge, and I stayed up one night composing and memorizing a host of conversational openers. First I would take her to see *Satan Never Sleeps* at the Plaza. I

didn't want to see *Satan Never Sleeps,* but I had scouted
the theater's parking lot and found that it would not
require parallel parking. From there, if all went well, we
would proceed to Belson's ice-cream parlor for a soda,
and then we would head for the park.

I spent the afternoon before my date rehearsing conversation in the shower, and when I got to the car my
fingers were still withered and waterlogged. "I know
you're going to be a gentleman," my mother called after
me as I backed out the driveway.

As soon as I got to Fredericka's house I struck Binney
Park from my plans. Fredericka turned out to be the
only sister of four older brothers who, standing with
their arms crossed in the hallway, gave the evening a
threatening, Maureen O'Hara quality. "I'll have her
back in no time," I promised as I hurried her to my
car.

I made a couple of wrong turns on the way to the
theater, but Fredericka didn't seem to notice them, and I
didn't even need my opening lines: she went right into
an involved account of a girl in chorus who had thrown
up during a rendition of "Ezekiel Saw De Wheel." But
when we reached downtown Stamford, Fredericka
noticed a parking space a few yards from the Plaza.

"What luck!" she exclaimed as I slowed the car.
"Now we won't have to park in that spooky lot."

I tried to stay calm, but already I could feel the night
giving way beneath me. There was no getting around it;
I was going to have to parallel park. I closed my eyes for
a moment, trying to visualize the little diagram in the
parking section of the driver's manual. I knew I was supposed to pull up beside the car in front of the space, and

I did that, but as I backed toward the space I turned the wheel too far.

"I — I think you're a little close to the fender, there," Fredericka said, and I jammed on the brakes, lurching her forward a little.

"So," I said, figuring that if ever I needed conversational openers it was now, "how about Miss Godenhaus? Isn't she something?" (Miss Godenhaus, my missile-breasted French teacher, had taken to devoting whole classes to discussions of her love life. "Roy is *so* marvelous," she told us, "but what am I to do? He never calls.")

"She's something, all right," Fredericka said, leaning out the window as I backed toward the space again, "but I think you may still be cutting it a little close out there."

Again I jammed on the brakes and straightened out the car. "And speaking of Miss Godenhaus," I persisted, reaching around and gaping out the back window, "how about that Mr. Stark? What a character."

This time I made it into the space, but at too sharp an angle, and everything I did from then on just seemed to lock me that way, with one headlight jutting out into the street, one rear tire jammed back against the curb.

For thirty minutes we sat in that car, rocking back and forth, edging closer to the curb, then farther from the curb, then closer, then farther. At one point I turned off the ignition and told her we were in far enough, and she got out and looked over at the curb and climbed back in.

"You're still out too far," she said, staring forward with her hands folded, and I started the car again and we rocked back and forth some more, minute after minute, and by the time I finally managed to bring the car close enough to the curb the Plaza's marquee had been turned off and we had to find our way to the manager's office to get our tickets. I had blown every line of conversation in that half hour, and as we drove away from the theater (the cars behind and in front of my space had disappeared) we couldn't find much to say about the movie, either, because we had missed the first reel and couldn't figure out what it was all about. So I skipped the sodas at Belson's, too, and drove her home in silence.

"Well of course you bombed," Ed told me the next morning. "She had the curse."

The Jerk

MY MOTHER WAS the only one in our family to come to terms with physical labor. The rest of us, if we couldn't get out of it, brought to it a misdirected ingenuity.

My grandfather was handy, and would never put up with more than the most peripheral assistance. My father spent much of his boyhood standing at the foot of a ladder, handing things up to Grandpa. Removed from the job at hand, my father took to wondering, with no special grasp of cause and effect, why his father couldn't patch the ceiling with window putty, or tilt the gutters by striking them with a hammer.

When he grew up, my father sometimes put his boyhood speculations to the test. One night (he usually embarked on his most ambitious projects in the plausible

current of the night) he set out to lay a sheet of linoleum on a bedroom floor. Rolling it out and gluing it
down little by little struck him as tedious, so he hit on
the idea of turning the floor-sized sheet over and apply-
ing the glue to the entire underside at once. My image
of him then crawling under the rapidly drying linoleum
and trying, with lunges of his outstretched limbs, to flip
it over without attaching it, in part, to the ceiling, the
walls, himself, is one of my most precious heirlooms.

It was with this legacy in tow that I approached my first
job. Some friends of mine in high school had taken to
working as soda jerks in Belson's ice-cream parlor. Mr.
Belson was tight with his money and paid "the boys," as
he called them, the minimum wage. But my friends kept
showing up at school with their wallets bulging and a
mercenary glint in their eyes, and I didn't want to fall
behind.

So I showed up at Belson's one Friday night to be
broken in by a classmate of mine named Hugh. Hugh
was tidy and studious and worked at his job with brisk
efficiency. He never mixed up the order slips the wait-
resses slapped upon the counter, and assembled sym-
metrical sundaes and elegant, bubbling sodas in a flash. I
think I knew then, as I watched Hugh work, that I had
gotten myself in over my head.

My first solo shift at Belson's started out slow, and I
spent some time straightening my apron, sloshing my
scoops, polishing the soda nozzles, and calculating, to
the minute, how much money I was making. Finally, my
first order came in, a request for a slice of cantaloupe
and a scoop of chocolate with butterscotch topping. In

my eagerness, I interpreted this to mean a slice of cantaloupe *combined* somehow with a scoop of chocolate with butterscotch topping. The result was not pretty, but I figured if there were one thing this job was going to teach me, it was that there was no accounting for taste.

The waitress picked up my concoction without inspecting it and set it down before her customer. "You think I'm going to permit my young lady here to eat anything that looks like that?" he bellowed as his companion sank in her seat beside him. "You think I'm going to sit still for this kind of treatment?"

The whole night went that way. I handed out a sundae with Coca-Cola syrup splashed over it, and in all kinds of ways had it demonstrated to me that when it comes to food, people have no sense of humor. At last, Mr. Belson himself waded in and took over. He was a solemn, silver-haired man who liked to stick close to the cash register, keeping track.

"Now, watch me, boy," he said, removing his jacket and rolling up his sleeves. But Mr. Belson was so flustered by my mishaps that he had a lot of trouble of his own filling the orders properly, and didn't come off as the seasoned professional he had hoped to portray.

The shift ended miserably with Mr. Belson declaring, "The whole trouble with you is you don't have enough power in your cream." By this he meant that the CO_2 cartridge on the whipped cream dispenser had run low. So he decided to change cartridges, forgetting, in his hurry, to secure a crucial clip to the nozzle, thus sputtering himself from head to toe with whipped cream and raging backward like a snow beast into the kitchen.

I never got any better at soda jerking. I was always confusing sodas with sundaes, frappes with floats. Once, as the orders fluttered in, I panicked completely and, like a robot gone berserk, filled the same order again and again, lining the counter with mocha malts.

One of the fringe benefits of working at Belson's was that you were allowed to eat your mistakes. I thought this was a lapse in Mr. Belson's frugality until I realized that rather than encourage his boys to make mistakes, it discouraged them. By the end of the day, with sherbet smeared along our forearms, spattered cream souring underfoot, chocolate sauce drying like blood between our fingers, nothing could have been further from our minds than settling down to a dairy treat.

Mr. Belson was always lecturing his boys about overhead. "*Balance* your scoops," he'd hiss as I prepared cones. "Don't *stuff* them in there."

Once, I spilled a can of maraschino cherries on the kitchen floor. The floor had not been cleaned for months so I decided the cherries were a loss and began to throw them away. Mr. Belson, ever vigilant by the register, caught sight of me and rushed in. "What do you think you're doing?" he asked, pulling me away and tossing the remaining cherries back into the can. "You think these things grow on trees?" I apologized, but I figured the least I could do was rinse them off, so I picked up the can and headed for the sink.

"*Now* what are you doing?" Mr. Belson demanded to know.

"Just rinsing them off, sir," I replied.

"Don't rinse them off, for God's sake," he exploded, slapping his forehead. "They'll lose all their flavor!"

What with the spray of whipped cream and the gritty cherries, I lost all respect for Mr. Belson, and went about my job with sullen detachment. Friday and Saturday nights, Belson's functioned as the town's malt shop, though it lacked a jukebox and prohibited dancing. Youths were always coming in, combed and deodorized, and asking where the party was. In Greenwich, everyone between the ages of fifteen and twenty-two spent their waking hours trying to find out where the party was, and for some reason, we soda jerks were supposed to know. Often enough there weren't any parties, or, if there were, I didn't know about them, so as a kind of hobby I took to inventing parties and sending youths deep into the back country in search of them.

"It'll look like nothing's happening," I'd tell them, "but that's because they don't want cops poking around. Everyone's parked their cars a few streets away, see, and they've put in these rubber curtains to block out the lights." Imprisoned behind the counter, up to my elbows in pineapple crunch, I got a certain satisfaction out of imagining party seekers creeping up on slumbering cub executives.

The end came on a Sunday morning, one of the busiest shifts at Belson's, when worshippers from half a dozen nearby churches filed in for refreshment. Among these pious customers was a prim, myopic man who always arrived with a dozen or so of his Sunday-school pupils following behind like ducklings.

"Now, then," he'd say, squinting down at his young charges. "What sort of cone would you like this morning, Patrick?" And Patrick would ask, "What kinds do they got?"

"Well," the prim man said, nodding to me, "perhaps this young man can tell you." And so I would recite all twenty flavors.

"I'll have the chocolate," Patrick replied (most of them would have the chocolate), and then the man would turn to his next pupil and ask, "And what flavor would *you* like, Salvatore?"

"I don't know," Salvatore would say. "What kinds do they got?"

This process would repeat itself for half an hour, until there was such a backlog of order slips along the counter that customers began to leave their tables in fist-shaking rages, children weeping after them.

Something had to give, and finally, on what would prove to be my last shift, I hit on a plan. The prim man came in as always and again asked Patrick what flavor he wanted.

"I don't know," Patrick replied. "What do they got?"

I began to recite the flavors as before, but when I reached "rum raisin" I paused, leaned over the counter, and in a low voice said, "Confidentially, sir, we've been having a little trouble with bugs this week."

The prim man swallowed. "Bugs?" he exclaimed in a small voice.

"Bugs," I said. I told him that the rum raisin was giving us the most trouble because the bugs looked a lot like raisins to begin with. However, he was not to worry about the pistachio, or any of the sherbets; there were only a few stray bugs in these flavors, and I could usually scoop around them.

The prim man gaped and paled, and, shooing his pupils out the door, shouted something to Mr. Belson about The Board of Health, God, and The Catholic Knights of Saint George. Minutes later, I found myself out in the parking lot with my wages in my hand, and my whole life ahead of me.

Hey, Nonny Nonny

A FEW MONTHS AGO, I was listening to a tape I made of Ray Charles when suddenly, toward the end of the second side, a strained bass came on, singing, "I'm the man that built the bridges, I'm the man that laid the track./ I'm the man that built this country with my shoulders and my back."

It took me a moment to realize that the voice was mine, singing to me from my boyhood cellar bedroom some fifteen years ago. I had been given a tape recorder in return for some yard work, and every night for weeks thereafter I had hovered over it, perfecting my vocal style.

A few bars into the song there was a creaking sound and then my mother's voice came on, calling down the stairs. "Andy? Have you finished your homework?"

My voice returned, an octave higher, wailing, "I will, Mom. Just a *minute*, O.K.? *Please*?"

There was a pause, then the sound of a door slamming, another pause, and then my basso profundo returned. "I'm the man that built the power dams and oiled all the cars,/ And I laid down the cornerstone for this great land of ours." And there the tape ended, and flapped along the reel.

When I was in the seventh grade, everyone had to come up with an act for Eastern Junior High School's annual talent show. All the acts were auditioned in music class, and most kids pantomimed Spike Jones records or got together for unison renditions of Johnny Mathis hits. But I decided to do something original.

At the time, I could play (or thought I could play) two instruments: the harmonica and the snare drum. So when my turn came I got up in front of the class, set up my drum, and stood next to it for a while, playing a tremulous rendition of "Down in the Valley" on my Hohner. Then, when the applause subsided, I told everyone to shut their eyes and imagine, as I played the drums, that Hessians were approaching. It took some doing on the part of my music teacher to get my classmates to go along with this, but when they finally did I sat down and began to play a simple march rhythm — ta-da-dum, ta-da-dum, ta-da-dum, dum, dum. I started out softly, crescendoed, peaked, and gradually worked my way back to silence.

The act flabbergasted my classmates — "That was so *different!*" a girl exclaimed — and I was voted into the show.

The night of my show business debut I spent a lot of time pacing around in the wings of the auditorium stage, tightening my snare, Butch-Waxing my hair, and trying to quiet the rumblings of stage fright by punching myself in the stomach. I was set to follow the ominous Turk Tartaddio, who had a startling flair for the accordion. He was an enormous hit, and as he played his encores ("Lady of Spain" rendered in various dance rhythms) my own act seemed to me increasingly lame and eccentric.

At last Turk left the stage, and as I walked out into the spotlight and set up my drum, a few of his fans were still imploring him to play on. I only played a few bars of "Down in the Valley" and then hurried over to my drum and, as before, told everyone to imagine that Hessians were coming. There was a hush, and I began to play, but in my eagerness to get off the stage I got things all turned around in my mind and started out by drumming loudly: TA-DA-DUM, TA-DA-DUM, TA-DA-DUM, DUM, DUM.

Too flustered to apologize and start over, I tried to salvage the situation by playing an inversion of my act. I gradually decrescendoed, paused, and then crescendoed, and ended up as I had started, vigorously banging away — all of which created the illusion of Hessians setting off for battle, marching a little way, realizing they'd forgotten something, and marching back to fetch it.

My voice changed when I was in the eighth grade. For a while there I had been an alto in Easternaires, the junior high school chorus, and sat among the girls, miserably singing the feminine parts of "Buffalo Gals" and "People Will Say We're in Love." But my voice began to dip uncontrollably, and I had to drop out of chorus for a couple of weeks until it steadied itself somewhere within the baritone range.

Music was hot stuff in the Greenwich, Connecticut, educational system: right up there with pep and football and button-down shirts. I joined every chorus there was in Greenwich High School — Senior Chorus, Sophomore Mixed Chorus, Allstate Chorus, Madrigals, Witchmen, Male Chorus, everything but Girls' General Chorus — and pretty soon Mr. Theodore, our maestro, was assigning solos to me.

The first of these was a spiritual — "Sometimes I Feel like a Motherless Child" — and I remember that when I stepped forward and began to sing, all my stage fright vanished. And when the chorus started to hum in respectful subordination behind my baritone, the hairs stood up on the back of my neck.

Of course, there were only so many baritone solos per year, no matter how many choruses I joined, so I began to toy with the idea of starting a folksinging group. There were already a lot of folksinging groups in my high school, most of which modeled themselves after The Kingston Trio. They all wore striped shirts and strummed guitars and sang in a breezy, barbershop style. After a sad song they'd get perky and say something like, "Never mind all that, you guys! Let's really do some singing!" and launch into hearty, hand-clapping songs like "Good News" or "Michael, Row the Boat Ashore." You got the impression that none of them ever had any trouble with girls, and that after the show they'd all go off and chuckle it up over some beers.

But it always seemed to me that singing was best

suited to expressing sorrow and longing, not high spirits, so my group was different. It was co-founded by a wide youth named Al, and the two of us drew in a keening tenor named Tom. We called ourselves The Wayward Three, a jaunty handle that couldn't have been less appropriate. Since Al and I were both bass-baritones, our sound was bottom-heavy, so that even when we tried to cheer up and do something light like "Jump Down, Spin Around" it had a dirge-like feeling.

We modeled ourselves not after The Kingston Trio, The Limelighters, The Brothers Four, or any of the other blue-eyed groups that were popular at the time, but after a solemn, barrel-chested trio of black men who called themselves The Phoenix Singers. They had an operatic approach to folk music and sang a lot of chain gang stuff with their shirts open. Come to think of it — and I can admit this only now that I'm married and have a son — you could name any black folksinger who sang with his shirt open and I had all his records: Harry Belafonte, Leon Bibb, Valentine Pringle, Joe and Eddie, Inman and Ira, and more.

We did everything we could to look like these performers, and even bought matching outfits at a clothing store in Greenwich. We couldn't find quite the right shirts. They should have been form-fitting with big lapels, but each of us was oddly shaped and all the store had were some brown button-downs. We bought ourselves matching black belts and pants, and would have looked all right if we had realized the incongruity of white socks and loafers with our repertoire.

We had better voices than the kids in the other groups, but we brought them to bear on some of the unlikeliest material. I don't think it ever occurred to us how we must have appeared belting chain gang songs. We might have overcome the gap between our material and our lives if we'd been willing to work out some choreography, but Tom and I couldn't even box-step. None of us played instruments, so all we could do was stand there, singing. Even that wasn't easy; all three of us had trouble looking our audiences in the face. Tom and I were underweight, and used to sing to the floor to make our necks look thicker, just as Al was overweight and sang to the ceiling to stretch his jowls. We tried to sing with our shirts open, but Tom and I were chestless, and our shirts would simply flap about, like curtains to a cave.

I don't think we ever made any money. I know we never made enough to make up for our costumes or the embossed calling cards we had printed. The most we would ever be promised was a lot of exposure or all the iced tea we could drink.

Our first job was at a Strawberry Festival Tom's mother had organized. It was held on a Saturday in the basement of a local church, and everyone was charged a couple of dollars for all the strawberries they could eat, with the proceeds going to a summer camp the church was sponsoring. But the strawberries never arrived, and when we got there to perform, everyone was angrily eating stacks of French toast.

No stage had been provided for us, so we wound up having to perform standing on one end of the condiment table, and since the ceiling was low, the three of us had to sing from a crouch. People quieted down and watched, their cheeks bulging, as we climbed up onto the table, but we lost them right away by starting off with a somber ballad. In the middle of our second number, an upbeat calypso steal from The Phoenix Singers' first album, a small boy spilled honey over my shoe, and all through our performance people kept reaching around us for jam and syrup and iced butter squares.

Al had tried to develop some patter to fill in the gaps between songs, and said things like, "Thank you, folks. You're very nice. We appreciate it," even when there was no applause. "Now we'd like to do a little thing for you we're kinda thrilled with, and we just hope you enjoy it half as much as we like singing it for you. Ready, guys? Here we go."

We went into a civil rights number — I think it was "O Freedom" — and Al began to exhort our audience to clap along, sing along, give some indication they were out there, listening. But only Tom's mother responded, and during the third verse a smiling man in a yachting cap came up to Tom and began to tug on his trouser leg. We tried to ignore him for a few bars, but finally all three of us stopped singing and leaned toward him to see what he wanted. "Say, fellas," he said cheerfully, "you got any idea where they keep the head around here?"

We had the opposite experience at a beach party on the outskirts of Stamford. It was the only job we had managed to drum up on our own. The host had picked up one of our calling cards in a local music shop. "I like your handle," he said when he called me. "Look, I don't gamble with my money. I never heard you guys, so I can't pay you anything. But I can guarantee you that if my brother shows you'll get exposure. He was in the business for a number of years, and if he likes your act, he'll give you contacts."

We went along with all that, and arrived in our matching outfits one Friday night. The party was held on a neighborhood beach, and all the guests seemed to be tenuously married couples. A bonfire had been lit, and when we stepped forward to sing, everyone was lying around, sullenly digging for beers in Styrofoam freezer chests. When we started singing our voices sounded thin in the breeze from the shore, and we had to lean close together to hear each other. But soon after we started, a hard blonde in pink pedal-pushers began to writhe uncontrollably on the sand, snapping her fingers and shutting her eyes. "Hey, hey, hey, hey," she began to chant, rising to her feet and dancing around the bonfire. "Ooo, boys, that's the beat!" she exclaimed as she wriggled by us. "Keep up that rhythm, and don't let me down!"

This seemed to break the ice, and pretty soon everyone was dancing around the fire. One man picked up two garbage can lids and played them like cymbals as he wagged around the flames. It didn't matter what we sang — Scottish ballads, freedom songs, Dust Bowl anthems — it seemed to drive everyone into an orgiastic frenzy. At one point a request was made for "Yellow Bird" by a paunchy man in Cannon towelling. None of us knew the words to "Yellow Bird," so we had to sing the first line — "Yellow bird up high in banana tree" — over and over, as the conga line around the fire thinned out, and couples fumbled off into the darkness.

At the end of the party the host weaved up to us with a wincing look-alike he identified as his brother. "Hey, you guys were terrific. Sid here thinks so, too, don't you, Sid?"

Sid waved the three of us over with a furtive gesture, as if he were about to relay precious industrial secrets. "O.K., boys," he said in a boozy whisper, "this is it. I've heard a lot of acts in my time, but you guys take the cake. I'm gonna give you the best advice I got, and no kidding around — here it is. No matter what you do, don't sing crap."

We all stood there, nodding, waiting for more, until he finally looked up at us with a hurt expression. "Didn't you hear me?" he said. "I said, 'Don't sing crap.' That's it. That's the payoff.

"Hey," he said, angrily turning to his brother. "Where'd you get these guys? I give them the best advice in the world, and they just stare at me. No thank you's. No nothing."

"Aw, Sid," his brother said, reaching toward him.

"Forget it!" Sid shouted, rushing away. "Jesus Christ. You open up to people, and they walk all over you!"

"Sid's touchy," the host explained as we climbed into our car, "but believe you me, he knows show business. He wasn't a cruise director those two summers for nothing."

When we went off to college we disbanded The Wayward Three, and I developed an act of my own. I had taught myself a few chords on a rented Korean-made guitar. It had a warped neck, so I couldn't play the high frets, and the gears kept slipping and throwing it out of tune, but as soon as I put it in my lap and strummed my first E minor chord I was hooked. I made my way from

"Down in the Valley" through "Chilly Winds" into "East Virginia," until I could finger-pick "Fair and Tender Ladies."

My parents bought me a fancy Martin double-o 16 to take to college, and I spent most of my time in college hunched over it. Hour after hour in dormitory basements, echoing lavatories, resounding stairwells, I would back up my renditions of "Waly, Waly," "Shenandoah," and "Go 'Way from My Window" with major sevenths and minor ninths.

I never performed at Oberlin, but I would occasionally rise in social gatherings to sing "Try to Remember," a specialty of mine I delivered in a smoky, heart-breaking voice. A dorm mate of mine named Kugler used to exclaim, "Christ, Ward. With an act like that you can have any girl in the school."

But he never understood that singing wasn't enough, that I needed some sort of follow-up. I once tried to seduce a blinky, promiscuous girl by singing to her in a study carrel, and for a while there it seemed to work; as I warbled beside her she began to move in close and give me damp looks. But when I finished the song I found I couldn't quite let go of my guitar and wound up singing another song, then another, all of them slow and wistful, until finally she stood and said she had a big day coming up.

I ranked low among Oberlin's folksingers. In those days, a lot of emphasis was placed on authenticity, and my Belafonte arrangements were frowned upon. There were solemn girls who knew fifty-verse Elizabethan ballads by heart, and boys who could make themselves sound like scratched, 78-RPM recordings of octogenarian Delta bluesmen.

Every month or so in the 1960's, all across the South, ancient black men with names like Blind Lemon Pig Iron, Tennessee Pappy Pox, Hoptoad Willy Wetland would be rediscovered, dragged off their porches, handed guitars, and sent on grueling concert tours.

A lot of these men had been carnival singers and entertainers in small-town dives in the 1920's, and they never knew what to make of their new college audiences. They knew they couldn't play as well as they used to — many of them barely had any voices left, some of them even dozed off during performances — but none of this seemed to matter to the executives' children who craned around them at concerts and seminars.

Every year, Oberlin would invite one of these old men to perform, and for a day or two he and an officer of the folk club would wander around the campus, patronizing each other. Few of these old carnival singers could stand the solemnity of the place, and wound up their visits trying to get drunk, or making a pass, or picking a fight — anything to get the evening off the ground. But no matter what they did, everyone would just sit at their feet, nodding reverently.

One old man was so hard of hearing that in the two days he spent at Oberlin he never did manage to get his guitar tuned. He had once been a remarkable musician, but now that his teeth were gone and arthritis had crippled his fingers, he was reduced to slurring his way through interchangeable twelve-bar blues. He tried to make up for his limited repertoire by telling stories about his carnival days, but he spoke in a Delta dialect that even speech therapists couldn't have understood.

"Thankya, thankya. Asa song hat binna bug funna onna flan witta whole sang brunch. So's I say, 'Way, dotta. Happa slang thang pang, budon' mazz runta rizza, hey?' So sadonna rotisong . . .''

It's possible he knew that his audience was only pretending to understand him, and, by speaking gibberish, he was getting back at his fans for bribing him out of his hard-earned retirement. If so, he must have gotten some pleasure out of knowing that he left scores of imitative white boys mastering arthritic riffs in his wake.

Oberlin didn't give credits for guitar playing, and even if it had they could not have made up for all the courses I flunked. By the middle of my sophomore year all my probationary extensions had run out, and I was asked to leave. "Use this time wisely," the pipe-smoking dean had told me during our first and last meeting. "Try not to take this too hard. Try to think not that you've failed us, or your family, but that you've failed yourself. I think that would be the most positive way to look at it."

I had slept badly at Oberlin, and things didn't improve when I got home. I found I couldn't sleep until the small hours and even then it was a thrashing, teeth-gnashing sleep. I'd wake up with my jaw aching, and sometimes I would have gnashed with such ferocity that my jaw would spontaneously dislocate, leaving me gaping and speechless until I could get up the courage to shove it back into place.

When I tried to look on the bright side all I could really come up with was that at least now I would be near New York City again, where I could try out my act on some real audiences. A friend of mine had told me about a coffee house in the Village which held an amateur night every Tuesday, and a few weeks after I got home I drove in to give it a try.

The coffee house was called The Mauve Scallion and had once been a top showcase for comics. But it was too small to accommodate the rock bands that had become all the rage, and was now reduced to booking declining folksingers with expired record contracts. When I got there, I was directed backstage by the manager, an invisible man who watched everything through a peephole near the stage and communicated through loudspeakers.

Talent Night, as it was called at The Mauve Scallion, was emceed by Bobby Bud, a slick, broad-shouldered, would-be singer who made his living modeling resort wear. When I found him, he was in a small room behind the stage, auditioning hopefuls. A massively built woman in a muumuu was playing a lute and singing an involved ballad about a homicide in fourteenth-century Scotland. The story line involved opposing clans, star-crossed lovers, and ghosts in the forms of horses, doves, cats, and bats, and even when all the principal characters had been killed off, the song showed no signs of coming to a close.

"Hey," Bud finally broke in, "that's great, honey. Really. But let me ask you something. You got anything a little more punchy?"

The woman gave him an offended look. "I'm not interested in what you call 'punchy.' I am trying in my small way to revive an art form that has been lost to us over the ages."

"Hey, I respect that. I really do. But I'm afraid punchy is what I need here."

"I expected as much," the woman said, angrily packing her lute. "I knew I could expect this from people such as you."

"Don't be that way," Bud said imperturbably as she barged out of the room. "Belt show tunes, and I'll give you prime billing anytime, anywhere. Now, who's next?"

I waited my turn for about half an hour, and watched as Bud signed up a comic named Tony Boffo who specialized in bosom jokes, a man who put tiny harmonicas in his mouth and played national anthems, and a damaged, tubercular boy who sang the blues and accompanied himself on what appeared to be salad servers.

"Hey, those are fun acts," Bud exclaimed, "but I need something slow, something sad, something with heart."

There was a silence, and I hesitantly stepped forward.

"You got something, kid?" Bud asked me. "You got what we're looking for, here?"

"I think so," I said, snapping open my guitar case.

" 'I think so.' Hey, everybody, did you catch that? Is that show business? Is that a trouper talking? Hey, never mind, kid. Let's hear what you got."

I figured that with his show-tune advice to the massive woman Bud would be a sucker for "Try to Remember," and after a few bars Bud broke in and said, "Where did you come from? Do you believe in miracles?" he asked no one in particular. "I ask for slow, I ask for sad, I ask for heart, and here he comes with the whole package. Hey, you're in, kid. I'm putting you after Boffo, here, so don't disappoint me. That's prime billing, and I don't hand out prime billing like it was garbage."

There wasn't much of a crowd that night, so I sat at a rear table to watch the beginning of the show. A waitress had been assigned to get the performers to purchase soft drinks (liquor was not served), and finally I ordered one and sipped it as Bud handsomely hopped up onto the little stage and began to sing. He had brought his own music along in the form of a record which the manager played through the speaker system. But when Bud finished his theme song, an uplifting number from *The Sound of Music,* the manager must have forgotten to lift the phonograph needle, because it went on to the next band, a cha-cha version of "My Favorite Things."

Bud grinned through his irritation, glancing up at the manager's peephole and snapping his fingers, and finally ducked behind the stage and lifted the needle himself, scraping it across the record with a spine-chilling noise.

"Hey," he said, leaping back onto the stage, "hi, everybody! How's it going, people? We got acts coming out of the walls tonight, so I think we're all going to have a happy. So now, without further ado, let's get on with the show!"

The harmonica man opened the show, and he was followed by twin sisters who sang a raunchy song in thin, air-hostess voices, and then Bud came back for a broad-chested rendition of "Over the Rainbow," and then Boffo came on. He was short and wore a flamboyant jacket with parrots on it and went on for several leering minutes about breasts. By the end of the routine he had scored few laughs with the audience, but had dragged in every bosom he could think of — his secretary's, his wife's, his mother's — and as I stepped up onto the stage to replace him he said with a desperate, last-ditch wink to the audience, "And get a load of the headlights on *this* one," pointing to me.

I was in good voice that night, and the amplification

from the loudspeakers seemed to relax me, because I played my arpeggios smoothly, and had no worries about forgetting the chords. I began to wonder if perhaps I could make a living out of singing folk songs, or show tunes, or whatever it was I sang, and, closing my eyes, I imagined that this wasn't Talent Night at The Mauve Scallion but Saturday night at The Bitter End or The Village Vanguard, packed with my loyal following.

I made it deep into the second verse and sang expansively, weaving my way up to the high note:

"Try to remember when life was so tender
   that dreams were kept beside your pillow;
"Try — "

But when I hit the high note — and I hit it without straining at all — I suddenly heard a cracking noise and found I could not close my mouth. I held on to the note for a time, repeating the chord beneath it, trying all the while to clamp my mouth closed. But it would not move, and finally, when I ran out of breath, I began to sing, ahhh, ahhh, instead of the words, trying to behave as though I were so overwhelmed by the tune that the words didn't matter.

I don't know if I got any applause. All I remember is rushing off the stage, still gaping, and standing in a corner of the club, hitting myself in the jaw as the waitress stood by, demanding payment for my Coke.

"Come on, sir," she said. "We can't give freebies to the performers."

"I ohhh," I told her, "ut I ot uhthing ong ith eye awww."

Pencils Down

EVERYTHING WILL BE GOING FINE, and then suddenly I will have that dream again, the one in which I am walking across a campus and a classmate runs by me, waving his arms and shouting, "Come on! You're late!"

"Late?" I call after him. "Late for what?"

"*Late for what?!*" he exclaims. "Late for Bretko's final!"

In spite of myself, I begin to lope after him. "Bretko? Who's Bretko?"

"Jesus Christ!" he says as we dash toward the classroom building, "where have you *been* all semester?"

It is just when we reach the classroom, where the final in a course I have never heard of on a subject I know nothing about is already in progress, that I wake up in a tangle of bedding, my eyes bulging like eggs.

The first real test I remember taking was at a solemn little pedagogic enterprise called the Lab School, to which the faculty of the University of Chicago sent its children and in which it tested out some of its educational theories. I spent four years guinea-pigging my way through the Lab School, but I don't remember very much about it. I do remember a wide, saintly kindergarten teacher who cured my stuttering. ("Now, take your time, Andy," she would say as I stammered before her. "We have all the time in the world.") And I remember Miss Mums, a siren of a second-grade teacher with a flamboyant bust who used to hop up and down whenever one of us answered her correctly. I still think the University was on to something when it hired Miss Mums; most of us did our best to keep her perpetually hopping before us.

In any case, sometime during the second grade a group of pale young men with attaché cases arrived at the school and established themselves in a little room which was usually devoted to hearing tests. We were called in one by one "to have a little fun," as Miss Mums put it, "with some nice big men." Some of us didn't want to have a little fun. One boy, whose mother made him wear some sort of prophylactic powder in his hair, fainted in the hallway when his turn came, and had to spend the rest of the day with the nurse.

When it came my turn, I walked down to the testing room and stood silently in the doorway, waiting to be noticed, which was my way of announcing myself in those days. I was finally beckoned in by a man with thick glasses that made his eyes look like fish suspended in ice.

"Now, Mark," he said brightly, "if you'll just take

your seat right here, we can all start playing with blocks."

Much too polite to correct him about my name, I took my seat at a table around which four men with note pads loomed attentively. I was given six red plastic cubes and told, with many winks and nods, to do whatever I felt like doing with them. In truth, I didn't feel like doing anything with them. I was old enough to know that you couldn't build anything with six cubes. But the men looked so eager that I decided to do what I could, which was to line them all up into a row, then into two rows of three, then into three rows of two. The three rows of two seemed to go over very big. I could see out of the corner of my eye that they had begun to jot furiously, nodding to themselves as if entire life philosophies were being confirmed before their eyes.

I shoved the blocks around a while longer and finally leaned back. There was a pause, and then suddenly one of the men rose to his feet agitatedly and jabbed his pencil into the fish-eyed man's ribs.

"See?" he exclaimed. "See? What did I tell you?"

"You never told me *anything!*" the fish-eyed man hissed back, shoving the pencil aside. There was a scene, and in the confusion I got down off my chair and made my way back to Miss Mums' room. "Now," she asked me as I sat down at my desk, "wasn't that fun?"

"Yes," I said, and she gave a little hop.

My parents seemed to have had me down for college *in utero*. I remember working on a geography report about Bolivia when I was in the third grade and my mother standing over me with an anxious look and declaring, "They're going to count this for college."

As far as she was concerned, they were going to count everything for college. She used college in her disciplinary warnings the way some mothers used Santa Claus. This had the effect of simultaneously trivializing and exalting my academic labors. On the one hand, I could not believe that my knowledge that Bolivia was the only country in the world to lynch two successive heads of state from the same lamp post was going to count for anything in college. On the other hand, I could sometimes imagine a tweedy admissions officer leaning back and asking, "By the way, Andrew, what country was it that lynched two successive heads of state from the same lamp post?"

"I believe that was Bolivia, sir."

"Excellent! Oh, excellent! Andrew, I believe you and Harvard are going to get along very nicely."

I never did very well in school; in fact, the further along I got the worse I did, until by senior year in high school I was just squeaking through. I ascribe this to a difficulty I've always had with admitting to ignorance. It is hard to learn anything when you are constantly trying to look as though you know it already. I would rarely ask a question, for instance, unless it was designed to demonstrate a precocious knowledge of the subject under discussion. I would always start off my questions with, "Wouldn't you say that . . .," knowing full well that the teacher would, and congratulate me for my insight. In what were known as bullshit courses, this worked in my favor. In math and science it got me nowhere.

My parents were perplexed by my performance in high school, to the point of commissioning a university testing center in New York City to determine what my problem was. Every Saturday for four weeks I made my way into the Village to undergo batteries of five or six tests at a sitting. I went in with my parents the first day, and we all sat around with a cheerful man who kept asking me what I thought of myself. I told him I wanted to be an artist, and had trouble studying. He smiled indulgently and said we would see about that.

I guess I've blocked out a lot of the tests I took in the following weeks. One of them was to check out my suitability for cost accounting. Another consisted of a series of paintings depicting ambiguous scenes which I was to interpret using multiple choice.

"The man and woman in the picture above have just:

    A. Had an argument.
    B. Made love.
    C. Poisoned themselves.
    D. Filed a joint return."

Another was a tricky test for artistic ability. There would be four drawings of, say, a circle placed in a square. In one the circle would be centered, in another it would be to one side, in another it would be to another side, and so on. The idea was to select the one which was most sound compositionally. I say this was tricky because at the time every artistic convention was up for grabs, and I could have whipped up a convincing aesthetic argument for any one of them. I decided, however, that the centered circle was most likely to suit the testing center's artistic soul, and my high score bore this out.

One of the exams was an oral I.Q. test. The tester was an earnest man in shirt sleeves who repeatedly told me to relax. "We're just going to kick around a few things," he said. "There's absolutely nothing to be afraid of."

He had me push blocks through holes, do something simple with some checkers, and perform various other tasks, and then we came to a part of the test where I was to explain to him the derivation of different sayings. This proved a bumpier ride than he had expected, because I had never heard a lot of the sayings he read to me. "One swallow does not make a summer," for instance, troubled me deeply. I had never heard it, knew nothing about ornithology, and stammered along for several minutes, operating on the theory that he meant the act of swallowing. I think I said something about the wine of life and the flask of spring, and I could see from the way my tester fidgeted that he had not been provided with contingencies covering my interpretation.

I can't say I didn't get anything out of all this. I was given some instruction on the ukelele by an old man in Washington Square during a testing break, and discovered a newsstand near the subway where I could buy *Gent* and *Nugget* without raising an eyebrow. When my parents and I were called back to hear the results, we were told that I was sharp as a tack, had trouble motivating myself to study, and should consider art as a profession. The cheerful man accepted my father's check for $125.00, and we all silently rode the train back to where I'd started.

I did pretty well on my English and history College Boards, and miserably in math and science, as was my pattern. My parents had me sign up for every testing date there was, and I swung at the ball in such varying locales as Danbury State Teachers' College, Tom's School of Business Success, and most of the high school auditoriums in southwestern Connecticut. One day, my mother saw an ad in the back of the *Times* for a College Board preparation class at a private school in the city, and in no time I was commuting again. It turned out that I was the only one in the class who did not come from midtown Manhattan, and the only male who didn't wear a yarmulke. The course turned out to be a fraud. The teacher, a shaky old fellow in gold framed bifocals, started off by informing us that there was no secret to doing well on College Boards, went on to talk a little about a sister of his who was about to undergo surgery, and then had us spend the rest of the time taking mock College Boards in exercise books we bought from the school for five dollars apiece.

Oberlin College was my first choice, naturally enough, because my parents went there, and my brother, and all my aunts and uncles, because my grandfather was head of its art department, and my father was one of its trustees. Oberlin had strict admissions standards in those days, and there was considerable doubt on my parents' part that I would gain admittance.

When I had my admissions interview in a hotel suite in New York, I had just received a D in chemistry, a course I had to pass in order to meet the science requirement, since I had all but flunked biology the year before. After several genial inquiries as to my family's health and whereabouts, the admissions officer proved remarkably encouraging. He hinted that I would be admitted

under what he called Oberlin's "Tom Sawyer Program," which permitted students with "asymmetrical
aptitudes," as he put it, to get in. He could not keep
from wincing as his eyes descended row upon row of D's
and C's in my high-school record, but he emphasized
and reemphasized the positive side: high marks in art
and English, soloist in the chorus, good attendance; and
as the interview drew to a close, I got the impression
that he was even more eager for me to go to Oberlin
College than I was. As he waited with me for the elevator in the foyer outside his suite, he held my coat for
me as I attempted, in vain, to get my second arm into its
sleeve. We waltzed around in this way for some time,
and as I finally stepped into the elevator, still lunging
about for my elusive sleeve, he looked at me with the
game, pained expression of a man at a dinner party who
must smack his lips over something repugnant.

Oberlin didn't turn out to be quite what I had in mind,
and vice versa. As I went along, I had more and more
trouble getting to class, until eventually I lost all track
of where I was supposed to be, and when. Sometimes I
would catch a glimpse of someone dimly familiar and
follow him to his next class, in the hope that it would
turn out to be one of my own. It never did turn out to be
one of my own, but in this way I attended some fascinat-
ing lectures on subjects ranging from a historical review
of the Albanian nation-state to the topical poetry of Po
Chü-i.

   I was well into my third, last-ditch semester at Oberlin
College before I finally managed to pinpoint my problem. I couldn't read. Not that I couldn't have stood up
before a Wednesday Assembly and read aloud from my

geology text in a clear, authoritative voice, making myself heard unto the last rows of Finney Chapel. It was
just that to my own ears I wouldn't have been making
any sense.

As finals week approached, I tried to overcome this
disability by locking myself into my room in the dormitory, laying out my study materials in the lone beam of
my Tensor desk lamp, and sitting there, hunched over
my open textbook with a yellow felt-tip pen ready to
underline important passages. I sat that way for hours
at a time, waiting for the words over which my eyes
passed to form phrases, sentences, ideas, and managing
only an occasional flicker of recognition, enough to link
perhaps twenty words together — "The exercise begins
a rather extensive study to be continued in later sections
of Chapter XXI" — never enough to gain me a foot-
hold.

I was reduced to hoping that it was all penetrating my
mind subconsciously, and I would tidily underline what I
could only assume was important — headings, captions,
opening and closing sentences, numbers, anything re-
sembling a list, and sometimes a central sentence, a few
of which, I figured, were probably important, too.

Underlining accomplished several purposes. It gave
me something to do, it demarcated the pages I had already gone through (I had no other way of knowing),
and it hid from whoever might duck into my room the
fact that I was, in effect, an illiterate, and had no business being in college in the first place.

My last final at Oberlin was in Geology I, a course I took
because it was touted to have been designed for the sci-
entifically inept. This touting did not, however, seem to

have originated with the Geology Department. If there is more to know about rocks than was included in Geology I, I don't want to hear about it. By the time I took the final, I had missed all but seven of my classes, and had received an F on my research paper, a study of the Greenwich, Connecticut, reservoir system which I had based on a water company comic book starring a character made out of drain-pipe named Wally Water.

I took the exam with some fifty other geology cadets in a dark, gothic room overlooking Tappan Square. The proctor, a work-booted geology major, handed out the test sheet and the bluebooks, and, stopwatch raised, signalled to us to begin.

The questions must have been mimeographed minutes before, because the ink still smelled sweet and dizzying. The first and second questions rang no bells at all, and as I read them my pen felt icy and useless in my fingers. In the third question I could barely make out the following: ". . . bituminous coal and discuss its suitability as a fuel. Use illustrations to explain your answer where necessary."

It was as if I had stumbled into someone else's identity. I didn't know anything about rocks. I didn't know anything about science. Why were they asking me these things? I stared up at the blackboard, where the proctor was already chalking up how much time we had left. He squinted back at me with suspicion, and I swerved my gaze ceilingward, as if searching for the appropriate phrasing with which to set down my brimming knowledge.

Coal. What did I know about coal? I thought of black lung, carbon paper, the heap of coal in my parents' basement in Chicago. Then, for a moment, a phrase sprang to my mind from an eighth-grade science text: "Coal results from the deterioration and mineralization of prehistoric tropical rainforests."

Quickly, before it sank back out of reach, I opened my bluebook and began to write. "Coal results from the deterioration and mineralization of prehistoric tropical rainforests. Coal deposits are apt to be found in those places where prehistoric tropical rainforests once stood. Thus, coal mines in present use are located in these places.

"Coal," I continued boldly, "contains some of the chemical elements of prehistoric tropical rainforests, but usually not all of them. Those that remain are those which have survived and, in a sense, resulted from, the deterioration and mineralization of prehistoric tropical rainforests."

That got me through three pages of large, loopy script. All around me, my classmates were filling one bluebook after another. One girl across the room wrote the ink out of one ballpoint, hurled it to the floor, and furiously scrawled on with another. All I could hear in the room was the steady scrape of pens and the rapid flutter of pages.

To drive home my point, I decided to deliver on a few illustrations. Carefully, but with a certain graphic flare, I drew:

1. a rainforest with arrows pointing to "trees," "scrub vegetation," "sun," and "topsoil,"
2. a rainforest deteriorating,
3. a deteriorated rainforest making its way underground,

4. a coal mine in full operation labelled "Thousands of years later," and,

5. a black lump labelled "resultant coal ore fragment."

These led to another drawing illustrating the chemical breakup of coal. I drew a circle and divided it into three parts, labelled "sulfur," "carbon," and "other." Coal was suitable as a fuel, I noted, because it burned.

As I underlined all my headings and captions I wondered about my alternatives. I could claim that I had overdosed on NoDoz, that I was reeling, hallucinating, unable to think. I could hand in a blank bluebook, copy out a C-level set of answers in another bluebook that evening, hand it in the next morning, and elegantly apologize for the mixup. I could feign a fainting spell or an epileptic fit or psychosomatic paralysis of my right hand. I could accuse the earnest, chalk-faced girl beside me of cheating and storm out the door, or punch out the proctor in a rebellious frenzy, becoming, overnight, a campus legend.

But it gradually became obvious to me that the college simply wanted me to answer these questions. Otherwise, I reasoned, they would not be asking them. And it was just as obvious that if I couldn't answer their questions, I had no business being there. Somehow, in the rustle of the testing room, this hit me like a revelation. I wanted to get up then, find the professor, and exclaim, "Say, sir, I didn't *realize* any of this." He would understand. It must have happened before.

I looked at two of my friends a few rows away, both busily writing. At these times my friends seemed distant and unfamiliar. They were each into their third or fourth bluebooks. What in God's name were they writing about?

The hinge of my jaw ached and trembled and as I yawned, the floor took on a soft, inviting look. I put down my pen and stretched out my legs and wondered if it would be all right if I just curled up for a little while on the scuffed, hardwood floor, closed my eyes, and slept.

"Pencils down," the proctor commanded, chopping at the air with his hand.

A resolute, perspiring girl in the front row raised her hand and asked if she could "just finish one last sentence."

The proctor nodded and a score of heads and hands ducked back down to finish sentences. I sat still for a moment, and then scribbled one last sentence, "Coal remains one of the most popular forms of fuel in use today."

"All right, that's it," the proctor declared, and everyone groaned and stretched and stacked their bluebooks. I signed mine with a bold hand, but glancing over my five pages I knew it was at last all over for me at Oberlin College. All that remained was one last explosion of red-inked exclamations expressing regrets, alarm, and grave concern for my future.

Tool or Die

WHEN I FLUNKED OUT of college I came home in an awful state, and my parents decided to firm me up by sending me off to apply for a job at a local machine shop called Thompkins Engines. Thompkins manufactured marine engines, or at least parts of marine engines. I never saw an assembled engine the entire four months I worked at Thompkins, just parts of various shapes and sizes. I didn't have any idea what these parts were for, and neither, it seemed, did anyone else at the shop. I worked with men who had been there for forty years without knowing, exactly, what they were making.

This gave the shop a disembodied quality, and most of the men worked in a kind of stupor. The shop was in a long, girdered, whitewashed building lined with ancient Pratt & Whitney machinery. The floor was composed of steel flecks, oil spills, and sawdust, compacted by dollies and forklifts and the lumbering tread of Thompkins employees.

I was started out at the deburring table, which was pretty much the bottom rung at Thompkins Engines. All *deburring* meant was filing off the little ragged edges, or burrs, the machines left on various small parts. Someone would roll a box of maybe five hundred bushings over to one side of my work stool and set an empty box on the other side. I would then take the bushings, one by one, out of the first box, file off the little burrs, and set the bushings down in the other box.

There were four of us at the deburring table: Julio, who commuted from the South Bronx; Willy, a half-witted Hungarian; Tony, a chain-smoking ex-machinist; and me. We found, after a while, that we didn't have much to talk about, and hours could go by without our exchanging a word.

Julio brought his radio to work, which relieved the tedium a little, but he would play only the Puerto Rican stations. Sometimes, to break the monotony, Julio and Willy would go through a furtive ritual. Winking at me, Julio would turn to Willy and ask, "Hey, Weelly. You gotta beeg jeeby-jeeby tonigh'?"

In response, Willy would rise to his feet with a whistling noise, grab himself between the legs, and exclaim, "Top this, spicky-span!"

"Oh, Weelly," Julio would reply, waving his file. "You don' be no sonamombeesh."

This exchange always doubled them over with laughter, and they repeated it two or three times a day.

I had trouble pacing myself at Thompkins. The day began at seven-thirty and passed sluggishly. I started out filing away with genuine interest in each little burr and thinking, "So this is how they make bushings!" But that line of thinking barely got me to nine, which was an hour from the morning break, three hours from lunch, seven and a half hours from home.

I tried switching hands for a while, then setting the file on the table and moving the bushings across it, then lining up several bushings and filing them at once, then using two files at once: just about everything short of filing with my feet. When all these innovations backfired, I began to visualize elaborate contraptions which would do the job at the flick of a switch: conveyor belts with burr sensors, carbide wheels, snatching devices to sort the bushings, automated dollies to cart them away.

At last the buzzer sounded, and all through the shop machines ground to a halt and men headed down the aisle to line up at the coffee truck. I bought three Danish, a candy bar, and two pints of orange juice, and downed as much as I could before the buzzer went off. But the older men, who knew better, returned from the coffee truck frowning over their change and sat heavily by their machines, breathing deeply between sips of coffee and little bites of Twinky. It wasn't until I had sucked up the last drop of orange juice that I realized I had spent more on my coffee break than I had made that morning.

As the machines resumed their whine and roar, I sat back down at the deburring table in a slump. Could this be only the first day of the first week of six months at Thompkins Engines? Six *months* of burrs and bushings and sonamombeesh?

"Hey, kid," Tony assured me, "you get used to it."

Tony was a scrawny, taciturn man who was missing three fingers on his right hand. A few years back, the shop manager, Mr. Patella, had installed a new public address system so that he could summon his employees without leaving his desk. Leaving his desk involved clearing everything off the top and locking all the drawers, which was a great bother. One day, Mr. Patella called Tony on the new system to remind him of an upcoming mandatory health exam. At the time, Tony was in the craft shop, cutting rods on a band saw, and he was so impressed by the sound of his name crackling over the P.A. system that after he had pushed a rod through the whirring blade, his hand followed after it, losing three skilled fingers in the process.

The P.A. system was removed, and Tony, who had spent twenty years working his way up to the craft shop, was put to work at the deburring table. To soothe his pride, Tony had developed a belief that filing was a tricky line of work and that every part he filed was worth at least fifty dollars.

"You see this lug nut, kid?" he'd ask me, squinting over his cigarette. "Don't look like much to you, but you figure mining, smelting, labor, transport, machining, and you got seventy, eighty dollars riding on this thing. So watch yourself."

Tony also took oblique comfort in the belief that Mr. Thompkins, the owner, was one of the richest men on the Eastern Seaboard. Thompkins wore shiny suits and drove a Rambler, but Tony insisted he did this to foil the I.R.S., and that when he got home he changed into silks and drove a Mercedes. According to Tony, when

Thompkins golfed it was only with important people, like Bud Collyer and Dennis Day.

At the end of each day, we were supposed to fill in tally cards and hand them to Joe Zykowski, the shop foreman. Zykowski was a wide, ambitious man who had taken a matchbook course in group dynamics and had been made foreman over the backs of several older, better qualified men. In the middle of my first week it dawned on me that if I were going to escape the deburring table I would have to impress Zykowski. The only avenue open to me was speed, so by my fourth day at Thompkins I became a blur of motion, emptying and filling boxes at a superhuman rate.

The others at the table began to glower at me over their files as I raced ahead. Willy, especially, liked to work at a leisurely pace, selecting a bushing, setting it down before him, flicking something off his knuckle, brushing his file, sighing, shifting in his seat. As I sped from box to box, he took to digging at the table with the point of his file, or, staring at me, grinding out his cigarette stubs in the palm of his hand.

"Look," Tony finally told me, cornering me over a break. "You don' work so fast. You slow down or we gonna get into lot of trouble."

"Oh, no," I replied. "Don't worry about me. I like to work fast."

"Maybe you don' hear so good," Tony said, shaking his chicken fist in my face. "You don't slow down, somethin's gonna happen to *you*."

My doubletime didn't go over very well with Zykowski, either. It meant he had to find more work for me, which meant more work for him. "What the hell do you mean, you're finished?" he'd exclaim as I handed him my tally card. "I just got you started on that job."

Toward the end of my third week at the deburring table Zykowski called me over to an idle drill press. "You think you can handle this thing?" he asked. "We're talking machinery, now. You screw up machinery, and I'll put you back in burrs."

"Top this, spicky-span!" I heard Willy exclaim across the shop.

"I can handle it," I assured him.

Zykowski called over an aging man with Popeye forearms. "This is Luzzi," he said. "He's gonna show you the ropes."

"O.K.," Luzzi said, wiping his hands with a rag. "We give him a try, Joe."

All the job involved was drilling holes in little steel cubes, but Luzzi demonstrated the job as if disaster lurked at every turn. "You pull the lever easy, O.K.? You watchin'? Bring it down easy, like so, all the way down till it don't go down no more. Then you bring it *up* slow. That's where you kids screw up. Bring it up fast and you'll shimmy your parts. That's no good. Bring it up slow, like I said, and you got somethin'. You doin' the job right."

Drilling didn't turn out to be much less tedious than deburring, but there was something about running a machine that gave it some dignity, and drilling was at least an emphatic job; each cube was altered by my work, and that seemed to make a difference.

My press separated two old men who now had to shout around me to converse. Their conversation was entirely dependent on aphorisms, which they could exchange for hours on end.

"Well," one of them would say, setting up his machine in the early morning, "like I say, where there's smoke there's fire."

"You said it," the other replied, leaning around me. "One hand washes the other."

"Yessir," the first would say with a sad shake of his head. "No fool like an old fool."

I had some notions about the nobility of the working man, and was drawn to Luzzi, who looked as though he had stepped off a Rivera mural. He never said much, but I hung around him during breaks, hoping he would let drop some nugget of worker's wisdom, something I could fall back on during future crises.

After a few weeks, Luzzi took to confiding in me. He told me he was having trouble with a brother who owed him money, and a daughter he was putting through business school wanted to quit and become an aquatic ballerina, and his mother was getting crazy and stalking through the neighborhood at night, rearranging lawn statuary. I never knew how to respond to these confidences and spent a lot of time just nodding and saying, "That's the way it goes, I guess."

Luzzi had a philosophical turn of mind, but he had trouble following through. One day, working his press, he told me life was just a cup of coffee. "You know," he said another time, pausing at his press, "drilling is like a lot of things." He didn't elaborate, and I just stood there, drilling, waiting for the full impact of his observations to hit me.

It is conceivable that during my months at Thompkins I drilled two hundred thousand holes. (I lost count after a few weeks.) Sometimes, toward the end of the day, I had to turn off my machine and sit down for a while,

convinced that the repetition was going to derange me
and I would be found blandly drilling holes through the
top of my hand.

I had applied to art school after flunking out of college and I was accepted for the fall term, so I knew that
my days at Thompkins were numbered. This set me
some distance from Luzzi and the aphoristic old men
who worked with me, but by the close of the day I felt
bound to them. I could see the stupor begin to lift from
their eyes as they scrubbed their hands in the long,
trough-like sink that ran the length of the washroom.
Under the spatter from the spigots, our hands, numbed
by the chill of the shop, would begin to bleed from un-
noticed cuts, and sting where steel flecks had worked in
under our skin. The blood and oil and suds would slip
past and gurgle down the drain as we compared our
plans for the evening: watching TV, reading the paper,
playing with the kids, taking it easy.

I made it through four months before I finally quit.
My doctor discovered I had a heart murmur and advised
me to give up heavy labor for a while. I guess that as
soon as I could afford to have mixed feelings about leaving Thompkins, I had them. Still, I was surprised by how
sad it made me feel to say goodbye.

"What do you mean, 'quitting'?" Zykowski said when
I broke the news. "I just got you started on a new job."

"I can't talk to you now," Tony told me, filing a little
rod as I paused by the deburring table. "These things go
for sixty, seventy dollars at least."

When I told Luzzi I was leaving, I realized I was
breaking some sort of code. "I didn't know anything
about this," he said, shaking his head.

"Well, I'm afraid I've got to quit," I said, putting out my hand. "But it was nice working with you."

"Yeah, well," Luzzi said, turning away with a distant look. "You weren't here that long, anyway."

Life Class

MY EDGIEST CLASS in art school was Life Drawing. It was part of the freshman program, which meant that everyone had to take it, no matter what his major was. The class was held at eight o'clock every weekday morning in one of the upper stories of a converted warehouse.

Life Drawing was taught by an elderly academician named Stoltz, who used to swoop around the class in a cape, flailing at feeble drawings with his cane. "You must dig *beneath* the flesh," he used to tell us. "You must go beneath the muscle, the bone, down to the very marrow, down to the very soul!"

This wasn't easy, especially with the models we had to work with. One of them, a Mrs. Reynolds, would always come in with a radio, a stack of fan magazines, and a box of bonbons and simply lie there on the modeling platform, putting on weight. Sometimes, gazing blearily at Mrs. Reynolds' spreading form in the chill of the studio, I would lose track of what I was drawing and have to retrace my steps back to her head, her feet, something recognizable, just to get my bearings.

An elderly woman named Madam Skyway posed with her legs clamped together and glared sharply around the room. When she thought she had caught one of the male students looking at her "that way," she became abusive, threw on her chemise, and flounced out of the class in protest. This so intimidated an earnest and bewildered industrial design major from Welcome, Minnesota, that his drawings became hazy wherever pudenda were called for and he wound up flunking the course.

The female models posed completely nude, but for some reason the male models were required to wear something minimal. One of these men was not a bad model — he had well-defined features and posed classically — but he had taken to depilating himself somewhere along life's highway, and kept his privates enclosed in a draw-stringed leather change purse. I could never figure out if he did this because he thought a jock strap would be distracting, or if this were his way of keeping track of his money.

The other man who used to pose for us had recently dropped out of a religious order and gone into modeling as a kind of penance. He was not one to just sit in a chair, or stand on two feet, or lie on his side. Instead, he would stand on the knuckles of his toes, or put all his weight on one finger, or mash his face into the floor and

remain that way, wincing, whimpering, suffering, until
Stoltz himself had to wade in and snap him out of it.

When Mr. Stoltz was laid low for a couple of weeks
with gastritis, an ambitious graduate student named
Phaedra Lanzafame came in to watch over the class.
Miss Lanzafame quickly concluded that what the class
needed was loosening up. "You're all so stilted," she
told us, clapping her hands together. "Come on, you
guys. Let's drop some preconceptions and have some *fun*
for a change."

So over the next few days she had us do things like
draw with our feet, fingerpaint, and, at one point, skip
around Madam Skyway to get a better grasp of her
"totality." This was something of a relief after Mr.
Stoltz, but it made Madam Skyway nervous. "Get them
away from me!" she shouted, lashing out with her
chemise as we romped around her.

In the class was a lean youth who had developed an
out-of-sorts, John Cassavetes style that went over well
with girls. His name was Yates, and he hated everything
about Miss Lanzafame. He refused to fingerpaint, or
skip, or do anything beyond sitting down, as Mr. Stoltz
had directed, and drawing naked people.

Yates fascinated Miss Lanzafame, and she was always trying to coax him into participating. "Come on,
now," she'd say, tugging at his sleeve. "You wouldn't
want anybody saying you were a pooper, would you?"

"You lay the hell off me," Yates snarled back, jerking
his arm away. "You can't make me do nothing."

One day, Miss Lanzafame decided to have us go off
to our rooms and return the next day with nude, life-
size studies of ourselves. "And this time," she said,

handing us huge sheets of shelf paper, "let's really go crazy, you guys."

This torpedoed whatever loosening up she might have accomplished by that point, but all of us, even Yates, went off and did what we were told. I decided to face the nudity issue head-on and deliver on a full frontal rendition, proportional down to almost the last detail, and after a shivering, narcissistic night in front of the mirror, I came in, like everyone else, with my drawing rolled up under my arm.

Miss Lanzafame had us pin our drawings up one by one, in alphabetical order. I had hoped that the assignment would satisfy my curiosity about the anatomies of some of my female classmates, but the ones I had wondered about most either drew badly, or skimped on details. As far as Miss Lanzafame was concerned, however, the assignment was a great success. "I feel I've set your spirits free," she exclaimed at one point, waving her arms around.

Finally it was Yates's turn to pin up his drawing, and a hush fell over us as he made his way to the front of the class and unfurled his masterpiece. It proved to be as well rendered as anything he had produced to date; however, it portrayed him performing an unnatural act upon the wishfully proportioned but unmistakable anatomy of Miss Lanzafame herself, outstretched on a tasseled divan.

This was more liberation than Miss Lanzafame had bargained for. Without another word she tore the drawing off the wall, rushed from the room, and, until Mr. Stoltz returned a few days later, left us to fend for ourselves.

Up the Hatch

"In heaven there is no beer."
Polish drinking song

GREENWICH WAS ON the New York border, and when I was in high school New York was one of two states in the Union which allowed eighteen-year-olds to drink whatever they wanted in public places. So every Friday and Saturday night the youth of Greenwich would rush across the line into Port Chester and Armonk to gather in special teen bars and get a buzz on.

My parents never cared very much about whether I drank or not. They didn't want me to overdo it, of course, or drive drunk, but you had to go back a ways in the Ward family to find a lush or a teetotaler, so drinking itself was never an issue. Perhaps this was why I never got into it the way a lot of my friends did. Rebellion gave their liquor an extra tang, and without it I could never develop any real momentum. I was always aware of how much it cost and how terrible it tasted; the manly transformation of pain into pleasure never appealed to me. So when I drank it was because there wasn't much else to do, because all my friends did it, and many of them with a vengeance.

My friend Munro was prematurely bald, and at fourteen he was able to fake his way into Port Chester bars. No one at such adolescent watering holes as Vahsen's, The Happy Tavern, or the Armonk Inn asked for his I.D., and he wound up drinking so much that by the time he turned eighteen he was already a reformed alcoholic. He still liked to hang around bars, however, and introduced me to the Kickoff Bar and Grill, a shabby out-of-the-way boozer a few blocks beyond downtown Port Chester. The Kickoff's proprietor, a circular, dyspeptic man named Val, preferred the patronage of derelicts to that of teenagers.

"Aw, hell," he'd exclaim to the neighborhood rummies slumped along the bar as we came in. "Here comes the sweater set."

Val was afraid that he was going to be swamped with teens, when all he wanted was to run a little corner pothouse. The owners of teen bars had to stock a lot of snack foods, and make space for dancing, and employ bouncers to deal with belligerent, inebriated jocks, and repair the nightly damage. Toilets were always being dislodged, windows broken, doors unhinged, chairs smashed. Worse, the talk along the bar was lightweight. It was one thing for a bartender to have to listen to full-grown men complain about their promiscuous wives, delinquent children, and capricious employers. It was another to have to commiserate with adolescents about their complexion problems, weekly-allowance cutbacks, and detention assignments. Teen bars like Vahsen's had a recreation room air, as if at any moment parents could swoop downstairs to put an end to the festivities. I think it was the atmosphere and not the management of such places that watered down the whiskey.

So it was Val's hostility and his taproom's seediness that drew us there. It made us feel more authentic, more debauched. The Kickoff was no more than a room with a bar, a TV, four tables with mismatched chairs, a cigarette machine, and a bowling game that was always on the fritz. The john, according to those who had dared to go in there, was something approaching the great abyss.

Among the regulars who nested along the battered, smoky bar were a retired hooker named Hot Rosa, and Lucky, an old midget who used to get smashed on straight 7-Ups. Lucky was a remorseful drinker, and every night he would wind up seated on the floor, crying, "Won't somebody keep me away from that old devil soda?"

Hot Rosa, however, drank the real thing straight out of shot glasses. She always wore elbow-length gloves, even on summer nights when the little room reached tropical temperatures. "They're my lucky gloves, boys," she once told us with an unaccountable leer. "I don't take these off for nobody." As the evening progressed, Hot Rosa's disposition soured, and she would lift her collapsed face and ask one of us how tall he was. "Oh, yeah?" she'd say when he replied. "I didn't know they could pile shit that high."

Rosa was usually the only woman in the Kickoff, but sometimes one of us would have the bad taste to bring a date. This always agitated Val, who had six daughters, and he'd call us over to a corner of his bar and say, "Don't bring nice girls into my place, for Christ's sake. What do you think I'm running here?"

If the date ordered a drink (most girls tended toward elaborate concoctions like velvet hammers and grasshoppers), Val would shake his head and say, "No way. It's too hot to mix. You can have a beer, but that's as far as I go."

We just couldn't seem to get enough of this sort of treatment. No matter how often Val short-changed and insulted us, we were always telling each other what a great old character he was, as we wove our way home along the Post Road in the early morning gloom.

Drinking and smoking had its romantic side in Greenwich High. Don Ghent, who was almost perpetually drunk, even in school, was revered by us all. It was said that he had already lost a lobe of his liver to drink, that one of his lungs was malfunctioning because of his chain-smoking, and in fact he did always appear to be nearing death's door. It was considered an indication of his delicate sensibilities that he was so crapulous, and Bianca Hogarth, a staffer on the high school literary magazine, was always trying to get him to write something. She had read somewhere that great writers were drunkards, and figured that the reverse must have been true as well. But Ghent would just stare at her, trying to get his eyes to focus, steady himself on her shoulder with one yellow, trembling hand, and wobble away.

Not all our drinking was done in Port Chester bars. Every weekend there were parties, many of them thrown by rich girls in the back country who desperately craved popularity. Their parents shared in their hopes and dreams, so most of these affairs were elaborately catered, and liquor flowed in extraordinary abundance. The trouble was that the guests at these parties tended to be strangers: bored, dateless boys with no stake at all in behaving themselves.

The evenings might start out decorously enough. Boys would arrive, sober and well groomed, canapés would circulate, and a few polite remarks would be made about the hostess's attire and the household's décor. But by the end of the evening one or the other or both would be drastically altered. Spurred on by booze and the contemptible bathos of their hostess's anguished hospitality, boys would begin to rage through the parlor, the library, the rec room, shattering the Wedgwood, tearing down the hunting prints, urinating on the Persian rugs, swinging from the crystal chandeliers. But such would be the intensity with which the household — the bewildered parents, the tattered daughter — longed for social prominence that as soon as the décor was repaired, the rugs cleaned, the pool drained, plans would be made for another party, which would wind up being even more elaborate, indiscriminate, and disastrous than the last.

Of course, not all parents were willing to put up with the wanton destruction of their property. Johnnie Wilkinson's parents finally got fed up with their son's weekly holocausts and hit on a solution that seemed to them perfectly sensible. They bought him a house. It wasn't much of a house, to be sure: just a little two-bedroom ranch house on the outskirts of Stamford. But it made Johnnie Wilkinson the toast of Greenwich, and became the site of parties that lasted all weekend, every weekend, year after year.

I came equipped with only two social gears — low and reverse — so when I went to parties it was usually as a spectator and sidekick. While revelers writhed around me I would stand in a corner reading liner notes, or admiring ship models, or hogging the dip.

Munro, however, had a glad-handing side that served him admirably at Greenwich parties. His precocious drinking had made him such a legend that he was welcome everywhere, even though he now refused all alcoholic beverages and sat among the drunkards sipping diet cola. Like me, he always went stag to parties, but unlike me he kept up a pretense that what he was really up to by crashing these affairs was trying to pick up girls. He had a smooth style at first which drew girls to him. He'd lean over and fix his eyes on them and say things in a mood music disc jockey's voice, but there was a serious gap in his repertoire: as soon as a girl expressed her willingness to dump her date and go with him somewhere he would suddenly look at his watch, snap his fingers, and feign appointments elsewhere.

One night a few weeks after high school graduation I accompanied Munro to one of Wilkinson's house parties. When we drove up around ten o'clock on a Saturday night we found that the party was already a day and a half old. The lawn was deeply rutted and everywhere cars were parked haphazardly. The house itself was dimly lit from the few wall lamps that had not been ripped out, and barren of furniture except for a couple

of befouled mattresses in one of the bedrooms. The
floors were so covered with beer cans that Munro and I
literally had to wade our way in. Wilkinson himself had
not been seen in twelve hours, but that didn't seem to
bother anybody. We weren't required to announce ourselves; people just wandered in and out.

Only a few people in the preliminary stages of inebri-
ation stumbled through the interior of the house, their
footsteps clanging like cow bells. The boy-girl ratio, as
at every Greenwich party, was out of whack, and a girl
in a black dress stood barefoot on one of the mattresses,
downing something from a Dixie cup as boys sat around
her, waiting for her to fall.

"Come on," Munro said, leading me back outside,
"the freak show's out here."

A lot of the cars parked helter-skelter in the yard still
had their headlights burning, which gave the night a
London blitz quality. Drunken youths stumbled into the
light, turned squinting and cursing, and lurched on into
the darkness.

"Well," I said to Munro, "I've got quite a day coming
up tomorrow."

"Jesus, Ward," Munro told me, "take it easy. What
are you afraid of?"

Among the things I was afraid of was Dom Morelli,
who now staggered forth out of the night with a colan-
der on his head and grabbed the front of my shirt.
"Hey," he wanted to know, "who's this?"

"He's with me, Dom," Munro said. "He's all right."

"Munro?" Dom said, frowning at him. "Munro? Is
that you?"

"Yeah, Dom. How they hanging, Dom?"

Morelli released me and put an arm around Munro's shoulders. "Hey, Munro. You're my friend. I'm your friend. Right? Ain't I your friend, Munro?"

Munro ducked his head. "Yeah, Dom. You're my friend."

"No, look," Dom said, as if Munro had missed the whole point. "I'm your *friend,* you know? You see what I mean? Like for instance . . . who don't you like here?"

"Who don't I like?"

"Yeah. Who's here that you don't like?"

Munro looked around the yard with a bewildered expression. "Hell, I don't know. I guess I don't care for Frontwick over there very much." Billy Frontwick, a freckled boy who did Bob Newhart routines, sat near a hedge, peaceably drinking peach brandy.

"Him?" Morelli said. "You don't like him?"

"Uh, no," Munro said with a shrug. "Not so much."

"O.K.," Morelli said, "whatever you say, Munro. You're my friend." And before we knew what was happening Morelli had marched over to Frontwick and kicked him in the side.

"Hey, Dom," Munro called out, but Morelli didn't hear him, and lifted Frontwick to his feet and reared back his fist.

"Well," Munro said, backing toward the car as the first blow landed. "Let's go get some burgers."

As we backed down the driveway a huge youth Munro recognized as Johnnie Wilkinson himself was tearing the door off somebody's car. "Hey, Munro," he shouted, pausing to wave as we drove away, "don't be a stranger!"

As I said, I didn't like liquor very much, but I actually hated beer. I liked the idea of beer, the look of it freshly gushed into a frosty mug, but it tasted god-awful.

I always drank beer in little sips, which of course made it taste worse, since it became warm and flat before I got through it. When my friends headed back to the bar for another round I'd beg off, claiming that I was into my fifth or sixth round already. I never got caught lying about this, but it gave me a reputation for imperviousness to alcohol that even I came to believe: a self-delusion that almost killed me during my last year in art school.

I was sent to art school because I had flunked out of college in my sophomore year and my parents didn't know what else to do with me. The school didn't accept any transfer credits (not that I had any credits to transfer) so I had to start all over again as a freshman.

I worked hard in art school, but my enthusiasms and my circumstances were always a little out of sync. Just as I had spent my few waking hours in college playing the guitar and taking photographs, I spent most of my time in art school reading biographies of American presidents. I majored in photography, and learned a lot, but the department emphasized the poetic and academic, and my classmates produced nothing but four-by-five contact prints of wet ferns, twigs in snow, gnarled tree trunks, closeups of vegetables, and gloomy, goosebumped nudes posed in barewalled student housing. I wanted to become a photojournalist, so after two years I figured I had put in my obligatory four years of higher education and decided to quit.

Around this time I began to go out with a tall, gre-

garious girl named Gwendolyn Hapgood. I don't remember how we got started. I was only drawn to girls
who didn't give a damn about me. That wasn't all they
had to have going for them, but it was an essential element. For five years I had been obsessed with a tiny,
unspeaking girl named Margo, whom I had briefly dated
in high school. Since Margo had never shown the slightest interest in me in all that time, my regard for her
never faltered, and I had been all but oblivious to the
vivacious girls in my art school classes.

But Spring hit hard my second year, enough so that I
forgave Gwendolyn Hapgood for actually liking me,
and we began to see a lot of each other. At first I didn't
know quite what to do with her. All my romances to that
point had been conducted at considerable distances.
Now, when it looked as though I were going to have to
kiss her on the lips, I would get this fluttery feeling and
tell her that since I was about to leave art school this
was no time for us to start falling for each other. But
Gwen cheerfully persisted, and I began to work through
my fluttering, and before the semester was out it looked
as though I were well on my way to relieving myself of
my shameful and burdensome virginity.

But as it turned out, Gwen and I were not made for
each other. As soon as I started to return her affection,
she got edgy and distant. It began to dawn on me that
she, too, was drawn to indifference, and that just as I
began to take an interest in her, she began to lose interest in me. Of course, this made her all the more desir-
able to me, and for many days and nights I wrestled with
this mutual exclusivity, skipping meals and dragging
after her as she contemptuously barked her commands:
"Buy me lunch." "Hold this." "Wait here."

It all came to a head one cold gray afternoon when I accompanied her to a year-end bacchanal at a classmate's house on the Rhode Island shore. Each guest was required to bring a bottle of liquor and a can of fruit juice, which were then to be emptied into a large plastic garbage can. The resulting brew, which had a pulpy, brown color, was the only beverage at the party and we scooped it up and consumed it in little paper cups.

The party was in full swing when we got there, and it looked a little like one of Wilkinson's revels, except that no one was ripping things up or kicking people in the side. Since most of the guests were art students, they tended to express themselves symbolically. One boy, a stenchy painting major who called himself Canadian Sunset, wandered cold and shirtless through the yard, holding a picture frame over his stomach, upon which he had painted a piny landscape backlit by an orange sun descending into his pants. A girl in textile design wore a flimsy garment and a spiky headdress which made her look like a promiscuous Statue of Liberty, and as the party progressed the tired, the poor, the wretched refuse chased after her along the teeming shore.

At some point I got separated from Gwen, and found myself stationed by the garbage punch, slaking my thirst. The brew tasted innocuous, like Kool-Aid, and I must have completely lost track of what it really was, or figured I was immune, because I downed cup after cup. I got into a heated debate with a boy named Banjo, and several people gathered around, scolding me for making value judgments. Just as I was about to make a telling point about the aesthetic bankruptcy of the new realism, I suddenly got the sensation of a great door slamming in my face. I staggered over for more punch, hoping an-

other shot would straighten me out, but when I downed
it I couldn't make any sense out of what Banjo was saying. It was as if his voice were coming to me on a tape
run backward. "I can't hear you," I told him. "What the
hell are you trying to say?" But Banjo seemed just to
keep talking, and the words still sounded babbled and
slipslapped. Music began to blare forth from speakers
set up in the garage, and I reeled toward it, jumping
slightly every few steps as if to catch the beat. The
music didn't seem to have any beat — it sounded to me
like traffic, or water gushing from a hose. But my jumping developed a momentum all its own, and I grabbed a
girl by the sleeve and pulled her to the driveway and
began to dance around her. I could see she was dismayed, or at least I could tell that she looked dismayed,
but I kept dancing around her, and then began to stagger
in circles away from her, off the driveway, across the
lawn, and fell into some reeds, clutching the swampy
ground to keep it from tilting, and throwing up what
little garbage punch had not been absorbed into my
starved system. By the time the host, a gigantic potter
named Revere, found me, I was convulsing, and an icy
rain was falling, drenching me to the bone.

Revere put me over his shoulder and carried me into
the house. Most of the guests had gone by then, and
Revere helped me undress and left me in the bathroom
for almost an hour to shower and regurgitate, shower
and regurgitate, until my clothes were dry. In all this
time there had been no sign of Gwen, and only when I
was led to the host's car for a lift back into the city did
she appear, expressionless and mute, sitting in the back
seat with her arms folded.

On the drive back into the city they had to stop a few times so that I could stand out on the roadside, breathing deeply and swallowing hard and trying to get my bearings. It was late evening by the time they let me off on my street. "There's your apartment, Andy," Gwen told me in a monotone as I climbed out of the car. "I've had quite a day. I'm going home."

There's my apartment, I thought as I stood wavering on the sidewalk, but where am I? Gwen pulled the door shut and the car sped down the street.

"Hey!" I heard myself cry out, stumbling into the street and waving. "Thanks everybody! Thanks for a wonderful time!"

With My Grandparents
at an Inn:
August 1970

WHEN MY GRANDFATHER goes out in the afternoon to rest on the lawn of the inn, he takes a lot of equipment with him: his cane, his cap, a sweater, a small blue plaid blanket, and a sofa cushion. His shirt, which hangs loosely from his diminished shoulders, flaps slightly in the breeze that slips across the lawn from the Connecticut River. The two breast pockets bulge with his paraphernalia. My grandfather never travels light, even on trips of fifty paces. He carries sun glasses and reading glasses, each with its left lens taped over to befuddle his double vision (one pair, in its case, to a breast pocket); two pens, one leaky and wrapped in Kleenex; a variety of pencil stubs with worn erasers; the small control box for his hearing aid; several carefully folded pieces of paper (lists, receipts, forgotten reminders); paper clips, pills, and a black eye-patch on an elastic cord. In his trouser pockets, each stretched and gaping from the overload, he carries a wallet, two handkerchiefs, loose change, rubber bands, more pills in plastic vessels, and a deck of credit cards in a leather billfold. His trousers are held up by a Florentine money belt, into which neatly folded fifty dollar bills have been tucked and zippered. All his life my grandfather has been a lover of gadgets; hooked up to his hearing aid, eye-patched, false-toothed, money-belted, an electric heart-pacer ticking beneath the flesh of his right breast, he has nearly fulfilled the ambition of becoming one.

Now he lies on his side in a low hammock. The small plaid blanket is spread across his legs to keep off the late-summer, late-afternoon chill. His head rests on a sofa cushion. He wears his eye-patch over his left eye and his cap is set at an angle to block the rays of the descending sun, all of which gives him a jaunty look. He listens to the rest of us talk — my grandmother; Debbie, my wife; and me — and he fidgets with the control box of his hearing aid, which was made by a now-defunct firm and is always breaking down.

I ask him why he does not buy a new hearing aid from a brand name company, and he glowers at me. He saves string, he files his correspondence, he still has blazers from his junior year at Princeton; he is not about to throw away his hearing aid merely because nobody has heard of it. The only trouble with it is a loose connection that can be remedied by wrapping fresh rubber bands around the control box.

His family is scornful of his gadgets and his discov-

eries. In hardware outlets, my grandfather is like a small
boy in a toy store. He delights in gadgets of multiple
use. Held this way, it is a can opener; turned this way, it
is a door stop. In his kitchen at home is his greatest
folly: a combination dishwasher and clothes washer. By
installing a dish rack and turning a lever to eliminate the
spin-dry cycle, it will do plates. He has stubbornly hung
on to this machine, though it dispenses lint upon his
glassware and coffee grounds into the pockets of his
trousers.

My grandmother sits on an aluminum lawn chair and
knits. Ever since I can remember, she has been knitting
sweaters, sun suits, scarves, and baby blankets for her
grandchildren. Whenever I was sent a sweater, she
would insist that I immediately report how it fit, how I
looked in it, where I appeared in it, how it was received.
My memories of visiting my grandparents feature pulling on sweater sections — a sleeve, a collar — while my
grandmother sat close by with her tape measure, taking
notes. Sometimes she would have underestimated my
growth rate by several pounds and inches, and I would
scrape my face with the harsh new yarn of a too-tight
collar.

My grandmother is aware of her faltering knitting
abilities. Instead of producing sweaters for her critical
family, she now knits cotton bandages for a leper colony
she read about. One of these bandages sits in a tight roll
on her lap.

I observe that both my grandparents have good color
in their cheeks. They protest that they do not have good
color in their cheeks, but are pleased to see that my wife

has lost some weight, though she mustn't get too thin. Grandma turns to me and says that before she dies she so hopes I will shave my beard so she may see my face again. Mention of my beard and her death in one sentence leaves me stammering. Grandpa declares that my beard gives me a dashing look, and besides, didn't her father, whom she worshipped, wear one? Grandma lowers her head, her eyebrows high, and counts her stitches.

Having established an alliance with me on the beard question, Grandpa inquires about the route I took to reach the inn. I tell him, and he breaks in with other routes I could have taken: shorter routes, prettier routes, less congested routes. Seeing her chance, Grandma tells me that while my route was not as scenic as the ones my grandfather is prescribing, it was probably every bit as quick. Grandpa reminds her that for the sixty years they have been married he was the one who knew the roads. My grandmother squints at her knitting and says it isn't important anyway. Grandpa now raises his head from the sofa cushion, his exposed eye flashing, and tells her not to contradict him in such matters.

This said, he lies back and looks regretful. During the next few minutes I fidget for new topics, but the matter of the route dominates the mood, and Debbie, unaccustomed to these disputes, is worried. After the longest pause, Grandpa reaches from his hammock and grips Grandma's forearm with the tips of his fingers, telling Debbie not to be concerned with their tiffs: that their squabbles keep them on their toes and don't mean a thing.

The New Hampshire evening air begins to penetrate his plaid blanket and we decide to reconvene in a sitting room of the inn. My grandfather tells us all to go on ahead, not to wait for him; he'll catch up. We all hold back at first, picking up his sofa cushion, his blanket, and, over his protests, walk beside him. But after a few paces Grandma takes the lead. She is so stooped over now, her rapid gait seems to be all that keeps her from pitching forward onto the grass. Grandpa, who likes to provide the momentum in most situations, watches her sternly, tells her to straighten up, tells her to watch her step or she will fall down and break her hip and there will be a fine end to their holiday. But she continues on with her knitting bag drooping low from one hand and she holds the door open for him as he makes his way across the patio, past retired bankers, a vacationing pair of ex-librarians, an old admiral, and a stray and restless young couple staying the night while their car is repaired.

My grandfather stops and introduces himself to the young couple, tells them that they can expect excellent food here, that he is a professor of art history, now retired, that this is his grandson come all the way from New York just to see his old grandfather. The young man wears a polo shirt and plaid knit slacks, his wife's hair is a precarious beehive, and they nod to me warily, taking in my jeans, beard, boots. We are in uniforms of armies my grandfather does not recognize. The couple seems dismayed by Grandpa, and only after he steps into the inn does the husband lean toward me to say that my grandfather seems like a friendly old guy.

Once, while driving my grandparents from their

home in Ohio to this same inn, we stopped for lunch at a turnpike cafeteria. There, at a crowded counter, the remains of the last traveller's meal still strewn before us, my grandfather introduced me, his wife, and himself to the harried waitress who had paused to take our order. As truckers paced behind us, waiting for gaps to appear along the counter, Grandpa went on to inform her of his profession, his place of residence, and his destination. She pressed us for our orders, gesturing plaintively at her other customers. Finally, with some further elaboration, Grandpa ordered our lunch. She wrote our orders down on separate checks and then, before turning to rush to the kitchen, she paused, looked at my grandfather, and then anxiously, as if defying tribal laws, told him that her name was Yvette Morgan, that she was a high school student from Buffalo, that she was seventeen and hoped to go to college. I wondered then if perhaps old men like my grandfather could be hired by the government as travelling missionaries to civilize the country.

My grandparents seem out of place at this inn; my grandfather has photographed the great cathedrals, lectured on the masters of the Renaissance, is an authority on colonial architecture, has designed and restored churches and houses, and directed a museum, and here he vacations with retired clerks and Dewey Decimal hasbeens who talk about nothing but cancer, menus, regularity, and day-to-day logistics: who talk about nothing at all.

We sit in the parlor, and I grow ambitious for my grandfather. My wife must hear him at his best. So I steer the conversation, so far no more worthy than that of the rest of the clientele, toward the architecture of the inn. He says he is growing forgetful and, besides, my wife would be bored if he got started. Of course we both protest, and he gradually warms to the subject. The moldings, he tells us, are additions, probably early Victorian, but the wainscotting, though not typical of the general period of the inn, is original. Everywhere he sees that the handbooks of Asher Benjamin were put to use by the builder, for the interiors of the inn are too sophisticated in their proportions to be the independent creation of a country carpenter.

Grandpa blooms with his knowledge, and I turn to Debbie with a proud look. This is my grandfather, and he knows everything there is to know about early American architecture. But Debbie is restless: startled by the clarity of his dissertation, but obviously not as transported as his grandson.

Nearby, my grandmother counts her stitches, her lips moving in the faintest whisper, and I feel alone with my grandfather. The hall has been reserved, the lecturer engaged, but I am the only one to show up. I try to make up for the poor gate by looking extra attentive. But where once I listened to him with awestruck fascination, loyalty begins to play a part in my concentration. I will listen to you, Grandpa; never mind the others. This element of loyalty is new, and, recognizing it, I see him grow frailer and more distant in his arm chair, even as he is animated by my stubborn show of attention, my questions, my challenges to his memory.

The owner of the inn, a vain man in his early sixties

who waxes his mustache and sits all day behind the front desk reading murder mysteries, enters the parlor now and asks if we would mind his watching the news. Grandpa, flustered by the man's entrance, agrees at once, embarrassed as if he had been caught in some foolish, private act. The innkeeper nods to each of us as the set warms up. He is wearing patent leather slip-ons and squints close to the screen.

It is a little past seven, and we have missed the lead story. The news is grim, bizarre: a plane is pirated off to a sheikdom, a mass grave is unearthed on the Mekong Delta, a deranged man has executed his family, demonstrators made up as corpses parade with a bloodstained flag. To my grandparents, the news is a fancifully staged event broadcast to pass the half-hour before dinner. But the demonstrators have angered the innkeeper. He wonders aloud what has become of the youth. Debbie takes up the gauntlet and replies that they are tired of the war. In my devotion to euphemism, I hope she will let the matter go, and I lean forward, my elbows on my knees, trying to concentrate on the commercial that occupies the screen. The innkeeper wants to know why if they're so tired of the war they help the other side keep it going. My wife does not believe they are helping the other side. The innkeeper says that is her opinion, and Debbie agrees.

We all sit in sullen silence, our shoulders high, as Eric Sevareid is introduced to tidy things up. He is overambitious for his topic — rising farm prices — and stretches his opening de Tocqueville metaphor to encompass every major news event of the past week. His

voice is soothing and, when he signs off, my grandmother expresses her admiration for his eloquence.
Eager for reconciliation in the parlor, we all agree.

A dinner bell is tapped and the four of us rise and head
for the dining room. As Grandpa walks toward his
table, he asks our young waitress what she has in store
for us this evening. She is his regular waitress and is
accustomed to his heartiness. She tells him he will just
have to wait and see.

Supper is the main event at the inn. My grandfather
has us discuss where each will sit and then clears up the
ensuing confusion by taking charge. The noise of silver-
ware against china is overamplified by Grandpa's hearing aid, so he takes it off and wraps the wire around the
rubber-banded control box. Then he takes out his reading glasses, holds them to the light, and wipes the un-
taped lens with a rumpled handkerchief. He spreads
his napkin on his lap, takes a deep breath, remarks out
of habit on the promising fragrance from the kitchen,
and settles into reading the menu card. In his infirmity
he seems to be working off a sensory checklist: getting
his hearing, sight, and scent into full operation before
indulging his faint, remaining sense of taste.

We have two choices: the lamb chops or the breaded
veal cutlet. Grandpa toys with ordering the lamb chops,
but Grandma persuades him that the veal would be
easier on his teeth. Veal it is, he tells our waitress, removing his glasses.

My grandmother begins to tell Debbie anecdotes
about my childhood. For instance, rising early one
morning at their house, I sat with her in the kitchen

watching the sun come up. She told me it was a beautiful sunrise and I said that where I came from — Chicago — we called them sunsets.

The meal is of small portions of soft food. My grandfather chews everything equally. He has been seen to chew jellied consommé. He looks around at us with our clean plates and frowns. We should know better than to eat so fast, he tells us. Eating fast will give us digestive problems and heart trouble in later life. After all, what is our hurry?

The innkeeper's wife, a high-strung woman with a bullhorn voice, holds back the swinging door, wiping her pink hands. Have we enjoyed our dinner? she asks each table, and everyone praises the food to the skies. My grandfather, caught in mid-chew, nods his head and vigorously points at his plate.

When we are finished, we fold our napkins and head for their room upstairs. Grandma careens ahead with Debbie, and I hold back with Grandpa. There are fifteen steep stairs and he must pause on the seventh to catch his breath. He waves me on ahead. I object, but he grips my arm and pushes me forward. He takes the last stair slowly, steadying himself on the banister, and his face is drained of color when he reaches the landing.

In their room Grandma has seated herself in front of a jigsaw puzzle. As my grandfather sits on his bed, I signal to Debbie that we will stay only a few more minutes.

I join Grandma and find a puzzle piece she has been looking for. It is the upper right sleeve of a blind and hunchbacked beggar, and it links two completed sections.

of a Brueghel Lenten scene. Grandma exclaims that I am wonderful, and I agree without hesitation. She gapes in mock dismay at my conceit and begins to chuckle. Aren't you the modest one, she says, ducking her head back down to study a monochrome corner of the puzzle.

Recovering from his climb, my grandfather turns to Debbie, who is feigning interest in a volume of *Reader's Digest Condensed Books,* scanning each page like radar. Is she religious? he asks her suddenly, and she allows as how she still is in some ways. He looks pleased and asks her what church she belongs to. She tells him Episcopal. Ah, he says, a Catholic who has flunked his Latin. Debbie laughs and admits that hers is a comfortable theology, but she loves the ceremony of the Episcopal church. She begins to recite the General Confession: she has done those things she ought not to have done and left undone those things she ought to have done. My grandfather joins in and speeds up the pace of the recitation until they are racing through it together, their faces bright with this competition of memory. When they are done, Grandpa asks her if she knows the old hymns. He begins to sing a Gothic one about Jesus at the door with his crown of bloody thorns, and Debbie sings along with him and knows every verse.

They sing two more hymns together, elaborate ones about lost souls, golden bridges, and the swift approach of the Day of Judgment. Each hymn is filled with doom and agony, but Grandpa sings them cheerfully, directing Debbie and himself with one upheld finger. They finish the hymn with a stretched-out cadence and sit back, still looking at each other with bright, admiring eyes.

My grandfather begins to talk about his boyhood, of

which these hymns are echoes, and tells my wife about his small-town church where during Sunday school he had been assigned to recite three psalms. Waylaid by the juiciest passages in the Song of Solomon, he had failed to memorize his lines in time and made a poor showing, stammering before the deacons, guilty and ashamed. He had promised himself that he would never perform so badly again, and from then on was always prepared for Bible, Latin, and Greek recitations, for any course of study depending on verbatim recall.

He does not tell the story as a lesson but as an explanation of himself. In his half-hearted retirement he has been plagued with doubts. Was he really a scholar, he wonders aloud, or did he merely like to collect information, as he collected stamps, postcards, books, and lithographs? Is he really religious enough to be a lay minister, or does he merely enjoy taking center stage before a congregation, showing off?

Grandma turns and scolds him for having such doubts, let alone expressing them. She tells him he was a great teacher, just as all his students said he was, and a fine minister, too. Grandpa stares at Debbie and smiles at her conspiratorially. These are just the ramblings of a sleepy old man, he tells her, and she mustn't pay them any mind.

I rise, work up a yawn, and announce that it is time we all got some sleep. Having refused their offer to buy us a night's lodgings at the inn, Debbie and I have decided to sleep in the woods across the road. Grandma says the New Hampshire air is too chilly, but as I kiss her I extol the virtues of our goose-down sleeping bags, and she is slightly reassured.

Grandpa sits on the edge of his bed and gives us a wry look. He remembers camping out when he was young, he tells us, and there is nothing healthier for body and soul, but Grandma points out that camping is not for old men with heart conditions. Too cheered by the hymns to argue, Grandpa shrugs and pouts in pretended consternation. We will join them for breakfast before driving back, I tell him, and I kiss him on his loose, abrasive cheek.

At the foot of the stairs we meet the innkeeper. We can see his wife setting up the tables for breakfast in the dining room. The innkeeper takes me aside for a moment and puts one hand on my shoulder, seeming to steady himself. My grandparents are old, he tells me, leaning close, much older than the others in the inn, and frailer, too. Maybe there's someplace around they could stay next summer where they would be better cared for because, the thing is, the insurance here just doesn't cover a lot of the things that can happen to really old people: breaking their hips, choking on their food.

He has been drinking, and perhaps he has taken me aside to get beyond his wife's hearing. I don't know what to say. It is between them and my grandparents, I want to tell him, but I say instead that I will take it up with my father, their son.

Just as long as there are no hard feelings, the innkeeper says.

No, none at all, I reply, shaking him off.

They're just getting awful old, he calls after us as we hurry out the door.

We carry our gear a few paces into the woods and pitch our tent on the forest floor. We fall asleep quickly, but deep in the night a thunderstorm awakens us, and we embrace until the lightning passes.